The Disaster of Resilience

Also Available from Bloomsbury

The Disaster of Resilience

Education, Digital Privatization, and Profiteering

Kenneth J. Saltman

BLOOMSBURY ACADEMIC
LONDON • NEW YORK • OXFORD • NEW DELHI • SYDNEY

BLOOMSBURY ACADEMIC
Bloomsbury Publishing Plc
50 Bedford Square, London, WC1B 3DP, UK
1385 Broadway, New York, NY 10018, USA
29 Earlsfort Terrace, Dublin 2, Ireland

BLOOMSBURY, BLOOMSBURY ACADEMIC and the Diana logo are trademarks
of Bloomsbury Publishing Plc

First published in Great Britain 2024

Cover design by Jess Stevens
Cover image © sampsyseeds / Getty Images

A catalogue record for this book is available from the British Library.

A catalog record for this book is available from the Library of Congress.

ISBN: HB: 978-1-3503-4241-5
PB: 978-1-3503-4240-8
ePDF: 978-1-3503-4242-2
eBook: 978-1-3503-4243-9

Typeset by Deanta Global Publishing Services, Chennai, India
Printed and bound in Great Britain

To find out more about our authors and books visit www.bloomsbury.com and
sign up for our newsletters.

Contents

Acknowledgments

A number of colleagues, friends, family members, and students provided valuable support, exchange, and suggestions that made this project possible. I am grateful to them. Robin Truth Goodman gave feedback on each chapter from conception to editing. Words cannot express my appreciation for her insights and time. Thanks to Bloomsbury Editor Mark Richardson for his support and thoughtful suggestions on this project. Rania Filippakou Giroux made helpful suggestions on sources. Thanks to Henry Giroux, Alex Means, Donaldo Macedo, Kathy Szybist, Simone Saltman, Hugo Rodriguez, Graham Slater, Enora Brown, Mark Giles, Kathryn Chval, Noah Gelfand, Rob Isaacs, Kevin Bunka, Al Lingis, David Hursh, and Mark Garrison.

1

The Politics of Resilience and Disaster

In the past decade, a number of seemingly disparate educational reforms, pedagogies, policies, and products in public education have vastly expanded. Though they appear to be different, they are united by a single concept, resilience. "The concept of resilience refers to the ability of social entities (e.g., individuals, households, firms, communities, economies) to absorb the impacts of external and internal system shocks without losing the ability to function, and failing that, to cope, adapt, and recover from those shocks."[1] Meditation, mindfulness, and growth mindset programs, digital educational apps, avatars, and games as well as behaviorist techniques and biometric devices purport to teach resilience to adverse social conditions while new cyber schools, education brokers (Uber-ed), global democracy promotion companies, supranational organizations, and dropout recovery firms promise school resilience to disaster and school disruption. *The Disaster of Resilience* examines the rise of resilience discourse as intimately interwoven with the new digital directions of educational privatization as well as cultural and political changes in schooling. Resilience has revived and revised disciplinary practices, paving the way for the new direction of educational privatization. Resilience promises the tools, mindsets, training, and skills for economic success while gutting humanities, social science, and other intellectual traditions. Resilience has provided the justification for new educational profiteering while fostering a cultural politics that individualizes collective responsibilities, depoliticizes and dehistoricizes knowledge and curriculum, and falsely grounds its politics in a mash-up of pseudo-science and human capital theory.

This book details how the now dominant role of resilience discourse in contemporary schooling undermines the democratic possibilities of public schooling. Resilience discourse continues and revises a number of long standing educational agendas that it purports to counter—particularly test-based accountability, standardization, a radical objectivism that disregards individual feelings and cultures. I argue that it is necessary to replace resilience discourse and its many programs with pedagogies and curriculum that offer students the tools not to simply endure and adapt to intolerable conditions but to understand them and collectively act to change them.

Forecast

This chapter details the varieties and uses of resilience discourse in the new directions of digital educational privatization, situating both in terms of broader economic, cultural, political, and educational antagonism and forces. The first section explains the rise of resilience assumptions and pedagogies behind the products and programs detailed in subsequent chapters—grit, meditation, play-based learning, biometrics, social and emotional learning, surveillance, and direct instruction apps and AI avatars. It discusses how resilience programs have been part of a global project spearheaded by organizations that represent global capital, the Organization for Economic Co-operation and Development (OECD) and World Economic Forum (WEF), to quantify student affect and behavior and create global learning standards. The quantification of affect and behavior via resilience framing creates the conditions for the commercialization of schools using digital educational technology. Some examples: the OECD, Lego, and Harvard have been collaborating to make play-based learning into a quantifiable and allegedly objective measure of student achievement on a global scale as Lego, the largest toy company in the world (headquartered in Denmark), has increasingly merged its toys with digital apps and educational products; venture philanthropists such as the New Schools Venture Fund invest in for-profit education apps like Centervention's ZooU that promise to teach social emotional learning skills of emotional regulation and self-discipline through digital games rather than through human interaction or dialogue. Education, media, and entertainment companies are increasingly cashing in on the expansion of resilience-oriented products in part through the trade in student data. During the Covid-19 pandemic, under the guise of school resilience to disaster, proponents of educational privatization used the disaster to repackage and promote a long-standing agenda to expand vouchers and "neovoucher" scholarship tax credits for funding dubious initiatives including uber-style private education broker schemes and cyber micropods.

The second section of this chapter situates the rise of resilience in education in terms of educational trends of past decades. Decades of standards and accountability movement tied to the global educational reform movement promoted heavy testing, standardization of knowledge, disregard for student experiences and cultures along with privatizations, and the expansion of corporate culture into education. The standards and accountability movement was premised on education as a neutral, quantifiable product that could be delivered more or less efficiently like any other commodity. Within the logic of this movement numerical measures of student achievement became sacrosanct and an industrial ethos of relentless control, measurement, and disciplining of students, teachers, and schools became the norm. Numerical test outcomes came to be equated with learning.

Resilience programs arose in direct reaction to the guise of disinterested objectivity, quantification, and disregard for human subjectivity in the standards and accountability movement. Resilience programs promise to attend to student differences, uniqueness, culture, and subjectivity that were roundly ignored by the long legacy of objectivistic standardized testing and standardization of curriculum and school models. However, as this section explains, they do so in ways that fail to acknowledge the individual as socially formed and capable of acting on the social world. Despite the rhetoric, resilience programs largely double down on the values, assumptions, and ideologies of the standards and accountability movement, repackaging them by misappropriating the language of progressive and critical education traditions. Rather than eschewing standardized testing, they aim to make testing ubiquitous. Resilience programs collectively function as an ostensibly kinder, gentler form of what Paulo Freire referred to as "banking education" that sees the student as an empty vessel and knowledge as deliverable commodity.[2] Resilience programs lubricate this delivery with a purported attention to feelings and experience.

The third section details how economic, political, and cultural forces and tendencies are driving these trends. Crises of capital accumulation on a global scale are pushing the pursuit of profit into everyday life in new ways. Resilience discourse functions as a kind of neoliberal character education that accords with and contributes to rising political and educational repression amid worsening inequality. As well, it details how the culture of resilience defines individuals atomistically by abstracting individuals from the social relationships that make their lives meaningful. In doing so, resilience discourse undermines social and political agency by treating experience as an effect of biology and undercutting the capacity of education to help youth translate private problems into public matters. The chapter details how resilience discourse is at odds with the elements of critical pedagogy, and it discusses why and how to move from the former to the latter.

Resilience is a growing global discourse that is being increasingly applied to multiple domains, including environment, disaster, economics, and education. Not only are supranational organizations such as the OECD, World Economic Forum, and World Bank promoting it in education but iterations of it can be found nationally and regionally for example in the UK Resilience in Education Programme, the European Parliament's Making More Resilient Education Systems, the World Bank's Protecting Human Capital in Latin America project, UNESCO's Resilience Project for Africa, to name a few. These programs largely share with the ones in the United States an allegiance to neoliberal human capital discourse, a promotion of privatization in the form of public-private partnerships, and signs of embracing digital educational privatization in the name of school system and student resilience to disaster. However, the United States appears to be leading the world in using resilience discourse as the content of for-profit digital educational products and using resilience to justify the datafication of affect and behavior in the interest of commercializing and privatizing education. For this reason, the majority of the illustrations of resilience for digital privatization in this book are US examples. The US context should serve as a "warning to the world" of a direction for the world not to follow.

Resilience Pedagogies

Resilience appears as a social goal globally in a number of different domains. As global warming threatens species and the planet, environmental resilience, resilience to disaster, and resilient cities have exploded as subjects of study. As economic inequality and social precarity have dramatically expanded in the past decades, the violence of poverty is met with projects that aim to teach individuals to be "resilient." Various resilience projects suggest that individuals can learn to withstand, survive, and adapt to brutal conditions: poverty, inequality, war, and psychological trauma. As the Covid-19 pandemic struck the world, schools, school districts, and students have all been hailed as needing to be more "resilient." Indeed, during the first two years of the plague a number of long-standing advocates of educational privatization made the case that resilience to disaster justified new privatizations.

Resilience appears as a nearly unquestionable virtue. After all, who can argue with the expansion of capacity of individuals, groups, or institutions to adapt to circumstances that they may not have made? Resilience now appears as a common sense good almost beyond question or doubt, embalmed in homey cliches and corporate marketing slogans: Stiff upper lip. Keep Calm and Carry On. Just Do It. Of course, as well, resilience accords with the long-standing ethos of self-reliance, character education, and meritocratic ideology that frames individual success as a matter of individual grit, determination, will, and gumption. Resilience framing resonates with biological narratives of evolutionary adaptation as well as social Darwinian cultural ideologies that celebrate the survival of the fittest amid harsh conditions and that naturalize human-made inequality through metaphors of nature. The promise of resilience appears also like an ancient narrative of heroic journey. The hero tested by adversity persists and prevails. As applied to schooling, resilience appears to be seamlessly woven into common sense, if not cliche: Who wouldn't want their child or student to persist in their studies? To exhibit grit? Who wouldn't want their school to adapt to challenging circumstances such as a pandemic?

Critical scholarship points out that the concept of resilience is in fact profoundly ideological.[3] Resilience as a concept began to proliferate as a value and virtue in the past forty years as social supports, public infrastructure, and the caregiving functions of governments became the targets of neoliberal restructuring around the world. Resilience not only asks of individuals and organizations that they become more adaptive to a harsher social world of shrinking safety nets, growing precarity, intensifying inequality, shuttered, privatized, and defunded public hospitals and schools, disappearing union work in high-skill, high-pay jobs, racialized disinvestment in cities, and a shift from funding the caregiving functions of the state to funding its repressive and punishing institutions—prisons, military, policing. Resilience also asks individuals to shoulder the onus for life outcomes and to accept the idea that their own capacities for choice, their own persistence and grit, would determine their futures.[4] That is, resilience promotes the idea that individual adaptability to allegedly unchangeable social realities drives individual life outcomes rather than recognizing how social forces, social structures, and collective actions produce the conditions for individual outcomes. As such, resilience promotes a particularly atomistic version of agency—that capacity to collectively act on and shape the world one inhabits. Agency under the aegis of resilience makes the self and private life the ultimate object of action rather than treating the social world or social forces as the necessary domains of influence. What is more, resilience goes hand in hand with other ideologies that, in the neoliberal era, redistribute responsibility for life outcomes from the society to the individual, including consumerism and discipline. In the context of redistributed responsibility and individualized security, the individual is expected to learn to manage risk in what Ulrich Beck referred to as "the risk society."[5] As Zygmunt Bauman pointed out, in the individualized society, as public health infrastructure has been eviscerated by neoliberal globalization, individuals are taught that they must be savvy consumers of gym memberships, supplements, and wellness programs.[6] As public education has been subject to the frenzied call for and implementation of privatization in the form of charter schooling, voucher schemes, neovoucher tax incentives, and growing digital privatization, parents are taught that they must be shrewd consumers of educational services who must cultivate their capacities to choose well or lose the competition for their children's future. Such centering of market choice as the essence of freedom displaces the public and democratic aspirations for free universal quality public goods and services.

As resilience makes individual self-discipline into a paramount virtue, people seek beneficial social outcomes privately in the self rather than in the society. To become a resilient subject of capacity one must cultivate self-discipline or learn it from a resilience program. Learning to be an adaptive self in the postindustrial neoliberal economy requires certain kinds of self-knowledge, self-regulation, and self-measurement that target the body.[7] Hence, the quantification of the self takes on inflated importance within resilience thinking. The resilient subject of health does not focus on reducing air pollution, eradicating junk food ads, or expanding public health programs. Rather she collects data, measuring steps taken, hours slept, calories consumed, heartbeats ticked. The resilient subject aspires for metrics that represent health security amid the risks to health that abound. Resilience pedagogies induce students to produce educational metrics that represent learning yet undermine the student's capacities to understand and act on proliferating social risks.

Resilience also tends to locate social shocks in the body for treatment rather than targeting the cause of the problem in the society and its structures. Hence, poverty, for example, is framed as causing physiological and psychological trauma that can be treated not by seeking to eradicate poverty for all, but by treating the alleged traumatic effects to the person through resilience training. In subsequent chapters, I detail programs that are alleged to treat this trauma, including grit pedagogy, meditation programs, mindfulness programs, and social and emotional learning (SEL). Such framing renders certain courses of action intelligible and others largely unimaginable. For example, if poverty becomes an individual problem with only individualized solutions, then broad-based remedies for it, such as economic redistribution, taxes on the rich, guaranteed income, universal provision of housing, health care, food, and education, all become superfluous. Instead, the solutions are sought in the terrain of the self: self-help, personal effectiveness training, financial literacy training, and so on. The effects of poverty seen in education, as well, are not framed as demanding the eradication of poverty and economic inequality but rather the need for resilience training for greater learned self-control, surveillance, affective tranquility, and behavior management. Such solutions address neither the systematic making of poverty nor the reasons for it. Reasons include state, legislative, and policy support for regressive taxation, the use of vast public money for the industries of war and repression, and precious little for institutions of care. More fundamentally, reasons for poverty include the maintenance of a hierarchical and antidemocratic arrangement for ownership and control of capital, monopolizing control and wealth extraction by the few, while subjecting most to the exploitation of their labor and extraction of their life energy and time.[8] As Fraser argues, contemporary financialized capitalism cannibalizes the very social and cultural reproductive forces that it depends upon including targeting for privatization and destruction public education.[9] These arrangements depend not only on force but also on consent, largely produced through culture which is taught and learned. Resilience is a growing and significant cultural pedagogy.[10] As a cultural pedagogy resilience discourse educates individuals into knowledge, values, assumptions, and identifications that inform how they interpret experience and formulate not just the solutions to problems but conceptualize the very problems themselves.

For example, countless nonprofit organizations, nongovernmental organizations, and governments trade in the concepts of urban resilience and environmental resilience, some doing projects like building housing, planning for future environmental disasters, or poverty reduction programs. While these activities in themselves are worthwhile and while these projects avoid emphasizing *individual* resilience, the framing of such programs through resilience participates in actively denying the very forces that produce the problems. Homelessness, global warming-induced environmental disaster, and poverty are consequences of capitalism. Capitalism depends upon exploitation and the expropriation of human and other natural resources. Resilience framing obscures collective comprehension of how capitalism produces these disasters, and it redirects human energy away from pursuing collective projects, politics, and ways of living that would pose the best chance of collective survival rather than adaptation to ever-worsening catastrophe—for example, replacing capitalist society with democratic, socialist, and environmentalist arrangements.[11]

New for-profit education technology products rely on the measurement and control of the self toward the end of self-management and capacity for adaptive choice. A variety of for-profit digital educational apps make resilience their content. The chapters that follow detail these examples, including biometric pedagogy, AI avatars, and the quantification of play-based learning. Consider, for example, products like surveillance app Class Dojo (that is now in the vast majority of US schools) that track student behavior and movement for teachers and parents, direct instruction app Amira Learning that utilizes an avatar to teach reading in a scripted fashion, and Centervention's Zoo U social and emotional learning app that purports to teach empathy and social relationships. All of these products were "incubated" at billionaire investor John Doerr's New Schools Venture Fund, which invested money in these tech startups.

These products have as their content the measurement and datafication of student behavior and affect. These app companies profit through contracting or other commercial arrangements that freeware allows. This data collection becomes the basis for commercial opportunities. For example, Class Dojo uses the information collected from students and families as part of "freely" sharing the app to then marketing social and emotional learning pay-for-fee mindfulness services to parents to purchase as supplemental through paid premium subscriptions. As well, the content of the products works culturally and ideologically in accord with the commercial perspective and broader neoliberal framing of resilience projects. Learned self-measurement for learned self-control for adaptation involves the quantification of the self toward the end of self-surveillance.

As the individual's capacities for choice and adaptation become of paramount importance, the activity of learning to control the self takes on inflated importance. Resilience programs merge a political-economic imperative for educational profiteering with a cultural politics of resilience in which the responsibility and onus for life outcomes shifts increasingly away from the state and politics and increasingly onto the individual and their cultivated capacities. They do so by making the student's behavior and affect a new frontier for data collection and commercialization while promoting neoliberal character education defined above all else through learned self-regulation, obedience to authority, docility and endurance of drudgery for standardized and meaningless[12] lessons, and empty slogans of self-optimization and positivity. Of course, there are winners and losers in such a shift. As the state abdicates its liberal welfare state functions, the state serves capital and social control by redirecting public wealth into corporate welfare, supporting corporate tax avoidance, reducing social spending, for example, on educational services, redirecting public wealth to repressive apparatuses including military, policing, and weapons production. Investment in digital resilience products on the one hand represents a new terrain of public spending on private for-profit contracting in schools. On the other hand, it represents an ideological and cultural project of reassigning blame for poverty, inequality, and social immiseration from the defunded social state to the individual who has either succeeded or failed to cultivate their capacities for resilience to worsening conditions.

The Rise of Resilience Pedagogies: How Resilience Expanded from Prior Educational Trends

To comprehend the development of resilience in education it is necessary to consider how it emerged from the dominant educational trends of the past forty years. In the 1980s public education was subject to a radical restructuring guided by neoliberal ideology and policy. The public roles and purposes of public schooling were recast through the language and logic of the private sector. Business rationales guided reform. Schools were described as businesses, parents and students as consumers of educational services, and administrators likened to corporate CEOs. Parents and families were supposed to be guided by consumer choice for schools. Schools were supposed to compete for parent/consumers. Schooling increasingly came to be described as needing to produce workers and consumers. This represented a sea change in how education had been conceived in the prior era as a public good necessary for not just workforce preparation but civic participation and humanistic ends. In the neoliberal era, the public role in education for democracy was displaced by the role of making economic actors in a capitalist economy.

The two most significant policy trends of neoliberal restructuring were school privatization and the related standards and accountability movement.[13] School privatization aimed to replace public schools with a private industry and to subject public schools to private market competition. This took form largely through efforts to undermine and close traditional public schools and replace them with privatized schools in the form of charter schools (academies in the UK) or private schools funded through vouchers or scholarship tax credits.

The standards and accountability movement worked in conjunction with the privatization movement to put in place testing regimens and curricular standardization designed not just to control and measure curriculum, pedagogy, and teacher work. It was also designed to defund and declare "failed" public schools that would then be subject to radical market experiments.[14] While privatization and accountability, competition and choice were the most pronounced reforms, numerous other market-based experiments and incessant denigration of public schools and the public itself were integral to this movement. For example, teacher pay for student test scores, modeling school districts on investment stock portfolios, busting teachers' unions, renaming schools for private academies, and having students dress as private school students or retail workers were just a few of many market-based trends.

Despite the incessant refrain of consumer choice, a crucial dimension to the neoliberal restructuring of public education was the expansion of repression. A key element of neoliberal ideology has been the suggestion that just as there is "no alternative to the market," there is no alternative to learning prescribed knowledge. Education is enforcement of the "right" knowledge from the "ones who know."[15] The neoliberal reform era has seen the expansion of militarized and prisonized schooling (particularly targeting working-class and poor students of color), and the standards and accountability movement presumes that good schooling is a matter of efficient delivery of knowledge demanding the disciplining of teachers and students.[16] Resilience discourse continues the trend by promoting programs and projects that target the body (and particularly working-class and poor Black and Brown bodies) for control and aim to educate the body in place of the mind. Whether it is the use of behaviorist training in grit pedagogies, the measurement of student bodies in biometric pedagogies, the turn to control of breathing in meditation programs, the quantification of affect in SEL programs, or the measurement and control of children in the quantification of play-based learning, as I discuss in Chapter 2, the body is the locus of control and the object of learned regulation.

From the 1980s to 2010 the neoliberal education reform movement relentlessly promoted privatization, competition and choice, the ideology of corporate culture, and a slew of market-style reforms. The Global Education Reform Movement was promoted by supranational organizations such as the World Bank and corporate foundations and sought to promote corporate management of schools and for-profit education development instead of universal free quality public education in poorer nations as well as test-based accountability, a business-oriented basic skills curriculum, and standardization.[17] In the United States, hard-charging corporate-oriented education leaders like Michelle Rhee and Joel Klein were celebrated in the media as willing to "take on the education establishment" and bust teachers unions, privatize, impose draconian punishments for failure to make test score gains, and experiment with a bevy of unproven market-based reforms such as "turnaround schools," "reconstitution," pay for performance "value-added assessment" of teachers, and "portfolio districts." The hard discipline of the market was framed as an antidote to the soft and inefficient public bureaucracy. Standardized test scores were framed as the only measures that mattered for quality. Films such as *Waiting for Superman, The Lottery,* and *Won't Back Down,* and NBC News pumped up chartering and privatization as desperately needed reforms, while political lobbying organizations such as Stand for Children, Democrats for Education Reform, and the Alliance for School Choice lobbied at the local, district, state, and national levels to expand caps on charter schools and replace traditional public schools with privatized ones, and all of these organizations and cultural products suggested that teachers, parents, and community members who defended traditional public schooling, defended teachers unions and secure work conditions for school staff, and criticized high-stakes testing were in fact betraying children.

Around 2010, as the neoliberal education frenzy peaked, a growing backlash began to break through the noise. The opt-out movement began to get national attention as parents, activists, education scholars, and citizens organized against high-stakes standardized testing, the tying of testing to privatization initiatives, and the undermining of public schools. The opt-out movement spurred parents and students to engage in open acts of resistance to standardized testing.[18] Parents and students individually and collectively walked out and refused to participate in standardized tests. As well, critics of educational privatization began to break through the public discourse.[19] Researchers, policy scholars, activists, union officials, parents, and many others began to highlight the failures of corporate school reform.[20] Vouchers were a particularly egregious engine of educational inequality, worsening the quality of schooling where they were introduced.[21] Chartering intensifies racial segregation and results in the push-outs of English Language Learner and Special Education students.[22] For-profit schooling, such as some charters and vouchers, resulted in the draining of money from the public system. Teachers unions, such as Chicago Teachers Union led by the Caucus of Rank and File Educators, began to link the defense of teacher labor and work conditions to the broader problems with both neoliberal privatization and broader social problems it produced like poverty.[23] Student movements such as those in Chile and Quebec demanded an end to privatization. Neoliberal reform and the standards and accountability movement, above all, were perceived as disregarding the individual student's culture, experiences, and feelings in favor of an allegedly objective, disinterested measure of educational attainment embodied on tests. That is, neoliberal accountability favored a kind of objectivism in which knowledge was framed as universal and impartial rather than partial and ideological, students were empty vessels to be filled, and the only issue was the efficient delivery of knowledge as if it was a commodity.

In light of the growing criticisms and problems with educational privatization and the standards and accountability movement, resilience discourse appeared to offer a profoundly new direction for school reform by seemingly shifting away from the guise of disinterested objectivity and toward student subjectivity, feelings, behavior, affect, and non-cognitive skills. Resilience programs focused on the importance of several key elements that appeared to break with the neoliberal ideology dominant for decades. "Non-cognitive skills" development was among the most significant of these.

The resilience emphasis on behavior, affect, and non-cognitive skills was developed as part of human capital theory dating back to the 1960s but really picked up traction in the 1980s and 1990s. Human capital discourse developed out of the work of economist Gary Becker at the University of Chicago, who was one of the "Chicago Boys" who worked with economist Milton Friedman, the "godfather of neoliberalism."[24] Human capital theory framed education as an economic investment and a crucial determinant of the economic development of national economies and the global economy. Human capital framed these educational investments not just in terms of knowledge acquired and skills learned but also affectual or behavioral dispositions. Human capital theorists, who were often econometricians, especially wanted to measure educational outputs relative to monetary inputs.[25] The dream of quantifying education as an investment would allow human capital theorists to look for the best "return on investment," cutting some expenditures that would not result in educational outputs presumed to create economic outputs and investing in those reforms that would maximize "return." As a consequence of the desire to quantify educational outputs to quantify economic effects, standardized test scores took on an inflated importance being equated with learning itself.

Human capital theory had an outsized impact on the growth of the standards and accountability movement globally as global organizations, including the OECD and World Bank, embraced human capital theory and aggressively advocated for educational policy in the name of economic development. Most significantly, they promoted test-based accountability and private for-profit development of public schools. Human capital theorists and these supranational organizations began in the early twenty-first century to increasingly link the measurement of non-cognitive skills to claims about economic development. As well, human capital theorists began to link their approaches to education and the economy to claims from empirical psychology about the physiological and psychological effects of poverty on the bodies of youth. In this narrative, poverty causes "toxic stress" and high "allostatic load" that result in blockages to learning. The solution for human capital theorists would not be projects to eradicate poverty as a means of reducing toxic stress and high allostatic load. Eradicating poverty would mean redistributive economic policies such as fairly taxing the rich, reducing economic inequality, expanding the public sphere social safety net for the poor, and policies that would limit the vicissitudes of capitalist markets, or better yet democratizing control over capital such that workers and owners are the same people.[26] All of these policies are at odds with the tenets of neoliberal economic doctrine that call for deregulating capital, cutting taxes on the rich, privatizing public goods and services, and shrinking the public role in ameliorating the destructive effects of capitalism. As David Harvey described it, neoliberal economic policy is a war waged by the rich on the rest.[27] Instead of aiming to end or reduce poverty, the solution for human capital theorists would be to make students more resilient to the poverty, adversity, and violence their neoliberal theories produced. This typically has meant dressing up as new, innovative, and technologically cutting edge, old pedagogies of learned self-control that employ techniques of behaviorism (found in grit pedagogies), teaching to the test (prominent in personalized learning platforms), and character education (found in social and emotional learning). It has also meant promoting a lot of unproven for-profit programs and jargon about mindfulness, meditation, and growth mindset as necessary investments in "non-cognitive skills" that would aid cognitive skills development and knowledge accumulation. And human capital theorists would increasingly seek to quantify non-cognitive skills. The long-standing project of quantifying affect and behavior has a symbiotic relationship with new commercial technologies such as AI, adaptive learning technology, biometrics, and learning management systems. These work by quantifying student behavior and converting student activity into data, crunching that data and selling these systems to school districts and governments. The promise of both resilience programs and digital tech programs is innovation and efficient adaptation.

Critics of human capital theory have pointed out that the theory mis-frames how the global economy actually functions.[28] For example, human capital theory assumes that higher levels of education produce greater levels of employment and economic growth. This has no way of accounting for the places around the world with extremely high levels of education and unemployment of the highly educated. In India, for example, half of engineering graduates are unemployed or driving taxis. Jamaica's economy was devastated by neoliberal structural adjustment policies imposed by the IMF/World Bank that required demolishing and privatizing public sector goods and services and redirecting public wealth to service high-interest loans from foreign banks. Jamaicans with university degrees found themselves working in "tax-free zone" where American corporations paid them pennies to do high-knowledge, high-skill marketing, and academic textbook proofreading.[29] This was the consequence of deregulation of capital and trade ("free trade") resulting in a global race to the bottom for the cheapest labor. That is, human capital theory is premised on a denial of the extent to which, in the era of financialized capitalism, global capital accumulation depends upon downward pressure on wages and efforts to defund tax bases that fund public goods and services which are prerequisite for economic growth. Human capital theory fails to account for the ways that economic development cannot depend on education alone but requires capital investment. In fact, as Fraser points out, contemporary capitalism pillages the very nonmarket supports on which it depends, such as public education.[30] As these previous examples illustrate, in places where capital was withdrawn or skimmed off for the further enrichment of corporations, banks, and rich nations, human capital became just another source of cheap exploitable labor. Human capital discourse furthers scapegoats and blames education for the poverty produced by capitalism. The human capital-inspired shift from the standards and accountability movement toward resilience discourse and projects is that the focus on the self has not been about developing forms of education that foster understanding the self and its relations to society or fostering the social and political agency of the self but rather controlling the self.

To get a more expansive understanding of why resilience programs
have both become among the most prevalent educational reforms and
why they have been at the center of digital privatization we have to
look at two kinds of motives driving these projects: profit motive and
ideologies of legitimation and social control. These imperatives driving
educational change must be considered historically.

Profit Motive

Neoliberal economic doctrine had its heyday from about 1980 to 2008.
Then, its deregulation of investment and mortgage markets produced the
global financial crisis that mainstreamed serious questions and doubts
about the model. As William I. Robinson argues, global capitalism is
characterized by boom-and-bust cycles as well as crises of capitalist
accumulation and state legitimation.[31] The transnational capitalist class
seeks new markets and, if necessary, makes them through destruction
and commercializing the ruins. Robinson refers to this as militarized
accumulation.[32] David Harvey, Nancy Fraser, and Michael Perelman,
among others, refer to this as "accumulation by dispossession" and
likewise point out that it is endemic to capitalism and ongoing.[33] When
most places have been colonized and commercially exploited, capitalists
commodify aspects of reality that have been hitherto unexploited. For
example, starting the in the 1980s, businesses began to see public sectors
as vast untapped privatization opportunities. In the aughts business put
public education in its targets, capitalizing on natural and human-made
disasters. Examples included using Hurricane Katrina in the Gulf Coast
to impose a vast privatization scheme and using the US invasion of Iraq
as a pretext to impose charter schools.

More recently, the private sector has turned to the lifeworld and
subjectivity itself as ripe to pillage.[34] Commodification of the lifeworld
is aided by the transformation of life into information and data in the
digital age. There are a number of ideologies that are deployed together
to justify the commercial exploitation of children through technology.
One ideology is that of technoutopian innovation: if technology, it's

inherently educationally beneficial. The absurdity of this view was nicely illustrated with the case of Los Angeles Unified School District distributing tablets to kindergartners and the young children writing on them with crayons. This long-standing technoutopian ideology was expressed in the 1980s with the idea that everyone in the future would need to code and so every school child was encouraged to learn to program in BASIC—a language that would soon be outmoded.

Public education, despite its civic and humanistic aims and overt public rationale, was a source of capitalist profit during most of the twentieth century and the era of the industrial economy. What sociologists of education refer to as social and cultural reproduction in education describes how education contributes to maintaining and reproducing the economic class hierarchy through the organization and distribution of knowledge, skills, and dispositions.[35] In the industrial era, schools taught skills and knowledge for the workforce and did so in ideological ways. The primary way that profit was made through public schooling in the industrial era was by providing, at public expense, knowledge and skills that would allow owners to hire workers and pay them less than the value of their work. The profit made by shortchanging workers was aided by the ideological lessons schools taught students slated for different roles in the economy. Working-class students learned basic skills but in ideological forms, emphasizing obedience to authority, and learned self-discipline, that knowledge and authority reside in the teacher, that one works alone, and that one competes against fellow students for scarce rewards. These lessons in school set the stage for the workplace where the worker would submit to the boss. Schools also taught different skills and ideologies to professional-class students slated for managerial roles in the public and private sectors. Academic preparation for university was paired with an emphasis on dispositions of dialogue, debate, and curiosity. For both working-class and professional students, public education represented a time- and labor-intensive investment in future exploitable labor.

The neoliberal era starting in the 1980s saw a number of changes to social and cultural reproduction as the economy was changing. The deregulation of capital as well as communication and transportation technology allowed for capital flight as industry moved production to cheaper locales around the world. Profits were sought through not just outsourcing production but privatizing public goods and services. Public hospitals, roads, schools, airports, and so on became subject to calls to privatize and let the "natural efficiencies of markets" do better than the hopelessly inefficient public management of public assets. In education the door was opened to allowing for-profit companies to manage schools through vouchers, charters, and scholarship tax credits. This allowed for-profit companies to collect public tax money and divert some of it away from the educational process and educational resources and toward the bank accounts of the owners of these businesses. For example, the profits of Chris Whittle, the owner of Edison Learning (rebranded from Edison Schools) which was the largest for-profit educational management company, came from the difference between per pupil spending by school districts and the smaller amount spent by Whittle on textbooks, teachers, physical sites, and differentiated instruction attentive to students' cultures languages and abilities. These profits allowed Whittle to live in a $95 million mansion, travel by private plane and limousine, and enjoy a gilded lifestyle.

For businesses looking to profit from public education, no longer was the long-term investment in training the future labor force the primary concern. Rather, quick profits through contracting arrangements became the focus. As the service economy of neoliberal restructuring shipped overseas high-paying, unionized, and high-skill jobs, it required basic skills and obedience of future workers. A growing number of students in the poorest communities were not expected to enter the workforce at all. Yet these economically marginalized students still represented a lucrative short-term opportunity for businesses that could get contracting arrangements for those students.

During neoliberal educational restructuring, the industrial era's values on learned self-discipline were increasingly accompanied by direct forms of control that less and less targeted the minds of students and the long-term process of ideological indoctrination. Increasingly in the postindustrial neoliberal era these reforms targeted the body. The prison which once aimed toward rehabilitation was transformed to lock away the body of prisoners. The psychoanalyst's couch which once required time- and labor-intensive therapy was increasingly replaced by antidepressant and antianxiety pills to manage the body and its emotions directly and immediately. The school which, in the Fordist era, required time- and labor-intensive ideologies of learned self-regulation increasingly shifted to more direct forms of bodily control.[36] This more direct form of control in education in the postindustrial neoliberal era has been typified by scripted lessons, direct instruction, rigid disciplinary codes of conduct with the threat of expulsion, the making of military officers and soldiers into administrators and teachers, the making of schools into military academies, the revival of behaviorism in the form of grit pedagogies, the development of biometric analytic pedagogy that targets the body, and the increasing quantification and control of behavior.

The new more direct forms of control are class-based and racialized. Working-class and non-white kids are targeted for police surveillance and arrest, scripted lessons, and other forms of repression. Professional-class and ruling-class youth must learn to be, in the words of Angela McRobbie (writing of postfeminist girlhood), to be entrepreneurial "subjects of capacity"[37] who learn to modify and modulate the body to compete for limited academic and economic opportunity. These youth learn to use attention and antianxiety drugs to compete by adapting to the drudgery of meaningless, standardized, and decontextualized knowledge. Resilience pedagogies, similarly, target the body and its affect with the promise of transforming youth into entrepreneurial subjects of capacity who will adapt to compete for limited opportunities. Not only is this a false promise but resilience pedagogies also need to be seen for what they displace (as subsequent chapters explain), including learning for social and political agency, knowledge that facilitates dispositions of interpretation and judgment, and curriculum and pedagogy that are critical and socially engaged. Resilience pedagogies also need to be comprehended in relation to other commercial endeavors that aim

at controlling working-class and poor non-white youth and adults—
especially the carceral industrial complex.

Resilience pedagogies represent a triple opportunity for investors
in the revised terrain of social and cultural reproduction during
the neoliberal era. First, they create new educational contracting
opportunities. This is the case of both digital and non-digital programs
that are enriching investors through contracts with school districts that
grab public tax money. Second, as curriculum and pedagogy become
increasingly digital and as resilience programs merge with technologies
that capture students' energy, impressing them into data production,
this creates opportunities for businesses to exploit this commercially
valuable data. Students become uncompensated data manufacturing
engines. Third, resilience represents a new education of students into
forms of learned self-control and ideologies of self-responsibility for
conditions not of their making. Resilience teaches social relations for
work in which endless adaptability to and endurance of worsening
contexts is portrayed as virtue, and character traits necessary to contest
injustice are portrayed as antisocial. As well, resilience represents an
extension of the big business in racialized repression (metal detectors,
security guards, biometric security, CCTV) that has steadily expanded
in schools for decades to warehouse and contain a growing portion
of the population that is superfluous to a postindustrial labor force of
shrinking highly paid high-skill jobs and the increasing automation of
work.

The next chapter offers several examples of resilience projects and
products and illustrates how they target the body for quantification and
commercialization and facilitate the expansion of digital educational
profiteering.

Resilient Bodies, Quantified Bodies

Making Students into Data and Money in Resilience Pedagogies

In the past two decades the student's body has increasingly become the locus of teaching and social control in schools. From the late 1990s school security has steadily increased in the form of police presence, lockdowns, metal detectors, and biometric surveillance.[1] Military personnel have been installed as administrators and teachers and military-themed charter schools have proliferated.[2] Not only have students been tracked, watched, measured, and controlled for alleged security purposes but students have also been induced to take nootropic stimulant drugs to game test scores and take antianxiety drugs to modulate social and educational competition stress.[3] Driven by social control and commercial interests and ideologies, control of the body has become integral to learned self-regulation for educational and supposedly future economic competition. Schooling has increasingly made the body the object of education. Some of the more glaring examples of this in the past decade include biometric pedagogy technologies, behaviorist grit pedagogies, and the quantification, surveillance, and control of affect in the form of quantified play-based learning, social and emotional learning, meditation programs, and mindfulness programs.

This chapter discusses how these resilience pedagogies call for students to misunderstand their experiences and emotions as either purely individual and subjective or as biological effects and radically objective. For example, meditation programs call for an inward turn away from the social conditions that produce experience. Alternatively, grit and other trauma-informed pedagogies assume experience is a biological effect of physiologic trauma that can be overcome by training the body. Proponents of play-based learning, such as Lego Foundation, position it as a necessary solution to the traumas of global conflict and yet advocate pedagogical approaches that do not address the causes of global conflict.[4]

As Italian philosopher Antonio Gramsci explained, the ruling group frames its particular interests as universal, disinterested, and objective interests.[5] This is evident during the neoliberal era with standardized testing, standardization of curriculum, and the culture of positivism claiming the universal imperative for students to learn official knowledge that is deemed to be impartial, disinterested, and apolitical. Testing and standardization conceal the ways that claims to truth and framing of knowledge are informed by the social positions, ideologies, and material and symbolic interests of those making the allegedly disinterested measures and standards. What is more, standardized testing and the accountability movement deny the extent to which contestation over knowledge relates to broader class and ideological antagonisms. Resilience, with its attention to subjectivity and feelings, seems to go against the guise of disinterested objectivity that has characterized the standards and accountability movement. On one level resilience programs appear to err on the side of subjectivism, making individual student feelings and behavior of primary importance in the educational process.[6] Were this the whole story it would be problematic in that student subjectivity is taken up in resilience programs in ways that disregard how subjectivity is structured and formed by objective social forces, structures, and antagonisms.[7]

However, resilience programs are increasingly being framed, particularly by supranational organizations, as in need of being objectivized, quantified, measured, and controlled. The aim is to make "non-cognitive skills" into a testable measure of students in the same way that standardized tests of reading and math are globally. That is, behavior and affect are framed in the growing global discourse of resilience as in need of being transformed into a disinterested, universally valuable measure or science grounded in other more established sciences such as empirical psychology.[8] This development of a quantified "science" of social and emotional learning is promoted by the supranational organizations, particularly the OECD and World Economic Forum. In the United States, the Every Student Succeeds Act (ESSA) codifies social and emotional learning—seeming to turn from objectivism and positivism to attention to student subjectivity, culture, agency, emotion, non-cognitive skills, and so on. *But* the new turn to subjectivity, experience, non-cognitive skills, and anti-testing posturing actually puts in place the opposite of what it purports to do. Resilience programs fail to relate the process of learning and objects of knowledge to students' experiences or to the social, political, and ideological forces that produce those experiences. Resilience programs may acknowledge students' emotions, but they do not provide the tools for students to comprehend what it is outside the self that informs or produces their feelings. For example, personalized learning is a depersonalized machine, constantly testing, with no acknowledgment of the connection between learning and culture or learning and the social context. Resilience programs depoliticize, psychologize, and thereby individualize social problems, obscuring class and cultural group antagonisms and naturalizing the existing social order as common sense.

As well, resilience pedagogies all aim to induce student self-control in the interest of making docile and compliant subjects who will consume prescribed knowledge and learn dispositions and ideologies of compliance for future exploitation in the workplace. Despite the appearance that resilience pedagogies are attentive to student interest and choice, they are universally wedded to transmission models of teaching and learning practices in which knowledge is framed as needing to be deposited in students. This runs contrary to constructivist, progressive, and critical scholarly traditions of learning that comprehend knowledge as co-created through dialogic exchange between teachers and students. Education in the resilience framework needs to be enforced. It is just enforced in ways that appear attentive to feelings and bodies but are not. All of this works well with the expansion of digital privatization initiatives as a much stealthier form of privatization that targets the bodies of students.

Resilience pedagogies that focus on the body do not position the social causes of violence as the central educational problem to be comprehended and addressed but rather focus on student adaptation to the social conditions. Learning and knowledge in this discourse become alienated from the social conditions that produce or inform experience. On the contrary, in the tradition of critical pedagogy, student experience needs to be comprehended as socially produced but also the reconstruction of experience can be the basis for social and political engagement. The corporeal resilience pedagogies criticized here set the stage for the quantification of behavior and affect through digital privatization and are also political ideologies that actively deny the politics of education, the cultural politics of knowledge, and the ways social antagonisms are experienced. As such they undermine the capacity for agency.

The first section reviews the array of corporeal and trauma-oriented pedagogies and their assumptions about student subjectivity, learning, and society. The second section situates the rise of these corporeal resilience pedagogies in terms of the agenda of supranational organizations to objectivize student affect and behavior to legitimize new deep forms of commercialization by the global corporations they represent.

Corporeal Resilience Pedagogies

Social and Emotional Learning

Perhaps the most widespread of resilience programs is social and emotional learning (SEL). SEL curriculum and programs have become ubiquitous in the United States, having been built into the Every

Student Succeeds Act that reauthorized the Elementary and Secondary Education Act by Congress. According to the leading organization promoting SEL, CASEL (Collaborative for Social and Emotional Learning), SEL is defined as follows:

> SEL is the process through which all young people and adults acquire and apply the knowledge, skills, and attitudes to develop healthy identities, manage emotions and achieve personal and collective goals, feel and show empathy for others, establish and maintain supportive relationships, and make responsible and caring decisions.[9]

SEL programs aim to teach self-management of emotion and self-control, interpersonal and relationship skills.

There is a great deal of slippage in meaning among resilience programs. For example, mindfulness programs that are similar to mediation programs are frequently described as variants of SEL. As well, there is a great deal of interpretation as to what constitutes SEL. In the United States as of 2022, there were SEL standards in place in nineteen of fifty states, all varying in terms of implementation and meaning. However, what appears universal in SEL are some key assumptions about the need for *learned self-control* of emotion, behavior, and affect for students to *adapt to existing circumstances* and social arrangements, and for this learned self-regulation to be the basis for expanded individual capacity of *responsibilized adaptive choice making*. The point not to be missed is that SEL programs, like biometrics, play-based learning, and meditation programs in their emphasis on adaptation to existing conditions, do not emphasize learning the social and political skills to interpret and act to change those circumstances. The fundamental lesson of all these resilience programs is that agency ought to be comprehended through adaptation, not politics, and that autonomy ought to be comprehended through accommodation and compliance, not active contestation of unjust social arrangements or conflict with the beneficiaries and architects of those arrangements.[10] Despite evacuating a social and political sense of agency, a large and growing number of resilience programs and advocacy discussed in this book co-opt and empty out the language of agency usually using it to refer to narrow student choices within a particular program that have no relationship to anything outside of the program.

Biometrics

Biometrics have increasingly become a prevalent resilience education technology. Biometrics measure the body. The data collected through measurement of bodies are used in education for a number of purposes. In past years the predominant uses were digital surveillance of students for security. During the Covid-19 pandemic, the security uses of biometrics expanded for automated test proctoring. Biometric analytic pedagogy collects data on a student's body and uses that information to make assumptions and interpretations about how biological effects indicate cognitive states such as student attention or inattention to the teacher and his lessons, interest or disinterest, or emotional response.[11] These teaching machines make a leap between what the body does and what the body means. For example, a student who might be looking at the door because they need to use the bathroom or react to someone entering the room might be the basis for a register of disinterest or inattention. More importantly, these technologies equate learning with physiological impact on the body rather than the mind as expressed by students through dialogue.

Biometrics technology transforms the process of learning into something akin to television commercial market research which measures the emotional stimulation of the TV viewer of a commercial in order to make lasting brand impressions. This technology functions as surveillance, control, and deskilling of teacher labor as teachers are measured by the physical effects on bodies and are induced to modify their performance in accordance with the measurements rather than based on reflection, dialogue, or theorization of the pedagogical scene. What is more, biometric analytic pedagogy has no room for the ways that students mediate what they learn, work through contradictory interpretations, raise questions, and engage in learning as an exchange with the educator. Instead, the teacher becomes a screen, and the student a passive viewer.

The Bill and Melinda Gates Foundation made headlines when they invested $1.4 million in researching "Q Sensor" biometric bracelets.[12] These sensors were intended to capture student's physical reactions to teachers' performance. Such biometric sensors had been used in consumer marketing research to gauge the effectiveness of advertisements in stimulating emotional arousal in prospective consumers. The Gates Foundation assumed that teaching as a performance ought to be measured by its physiological effect on students, their attention, their interest as measured by the body. The Gates Foundation also promoted the idea that quality education is a function of a single variable: teacher quality. And the project of measuring student bodies was really a project of measuring teacher performance. In this logic, only by measuring, controlling, and disciplining the bodies of teachers could teachers be forced to conform to imperatives imposed on them by standards. Once teachers' bodies were controllable, they could be replaced by programs and platforms—a move evident in, for example, "personalized learning" algorithms[13] and AI avatar reading programs (e.g., Amira Learning discussed in Chapter 4). As well, it presumes that learning and knowledge can be read off the body of students and that such measurements can quantify the efficacy of teachers.

Similarly, as I discuss in *Scripted Bodies*, a company called Affectiva developed a webcam biometric platform that measures students' faces in real time, analyzing changes in distance between the corners of the eyes and mouth. The software takes the data from the webcams and interprets the movement as indicative of attention or inattention to the teacher, positive or negative valence toward the teacher and the lesson. The promise of the product is to provide teachers and administrators real-time data that they may use to adapt their teaching based on how the performance is impacting the students. There are a number of practical and theoretical questions raised by this product. In a practical sense it is imaginable that a student being distracted by another student going to the bathroom would be read as inattention to the teacher's lesson.

As well, there is the assumption that how a student physically reacts to the teacher could be directly interpreted as indicative of learning. However, students don't simply absorb knowledge from teachers. They question, doubt, mediate, sometime agree with, and sometimes utterly reject what a teacher is saying in a lesson. The complexity of human response is not accounted for in this product. Biometric pedagogies reduce learning to a physiological effect on bodies and treat teaching as a performance that impacts student bodies. The bodies of students are interpreted as disinterested and objective measures of learning rather than, for example, comprehending thinking, conversing, or other language-based expressions of meaning. The bodies of teachers are interpreted in a machinic fashion enacting a scripted performance with greater or lesser fidelity evaluated by the bodies of students. Control of bodies trumps thinking and dialogue; transmission of knowledge displaces co-construction of knowledge through exchange.

Biometric analytic pedagogy expresses the logic of resilience. Students are measured and given data of the self to regulate themselves to adapt to educational conditions not of their making. Teachers are given data of students' biological reactions to their performance and are expected to regulate their behavior to game the metrics. As Chandler and Reid point out, resilience projects give students quantified self-knowledge to adapt, rather than to develop agency and autonomy.[14] Similarly, teachers adapt to imposed standardized demands instead of exercising pedagogical authority, creativity, and instead of engaging with the particular contexts and cultures of the students.

Grit

Grit pedagogy was developed in part by Angela Duckworth as part of the positive psychology movement. Grit aims to instill habits of perseverance in students. Task completion as a value is delinked from the value of the task. As Paul Tough explains in his book *How Children Succeed*, grit aims to make students resilient to adverse circumstances such as poverty that allegedly cause physiological and psychological changes to the individual.[15] The literature suggests that conditions of poverty traumatize the individual and reduce the individual's capacity for stress, which is referred to as "allostatic load." Grit proponents allege that the academic and life success of youth is compromised by the trauma of poverty and suggest that training in learned task perseverance can counter this, making individuals resilient. Grit proponents presume that poverty and inequality are unchangeable life conditions for some youth and that these social conditions should not be the target of change. Instead, grit advocates learned self-discipline to endure the drudgery of tasks that may not be terribly meaningful. Learned persistence in the face of drudgery in school will supposedly result in work and life success.

Duckworth reveals a telling dimension of grit pedagogy in her story of discovering the secret of grit.[16] She conducted studies with soldiers who were told to throw rocks from one pile to another for as long as they could. She recounts that what distinguished the grittiest soldier who would not stop throwing rocks from the ones who quit was that the persistent rock throwers reported an inability to imagine doing anything else except the task at hand. What is remarkable here is not only that grit as a trait delinks the value of an activity from the value of persisting in the activity. What is also remarkable is that the unusual lack of capacity to imagine something better is celebrated as a virtue to be taught.

In the context of education, grit pedagogy suggests that learning be conceived of as training: persistent repetition. Consequently, the exchanges between teachers and students involve a rapid behaviorist exchange employing visual cues. Learning is not conceived of as a process of reflective dialogue, the fostering of thinking, or development of capacity for interpretation and judgment. Nor is learning understood as a process that involves comprehending and criticizing injustice and oppression in the world to imagine and enact a better world. Namely, grit does not involve what Paulo Freire referred to as denouncing the oppressive dimension of the present in order to announce a better future.[17] Denunciation requires the intellectual tools of social criticism and annunciation requires development of the radical imagination. Grit appears to be designed to make obedient and compliant workers in a social context experienced as increasingly precarious. Yet, grit proponents frame their project as optimizing choice by cultivating universal habits of success. I have elsewhere termed grit "neoliberal character education"[18] because in a context of imposed economic austerity, worsening economic inequality, and financial crisis brought about by neoliberal policies, schools and students are scapegoated and blamed for conditions not of their making and subject to yet more discipline.

In a context of rising political authoritarianism, grit represents a dangerous demand for conformity and a rejection of ethical reflection on the value and implications of obedient action. It also represents a demand for dispositions that are thoroughly at odds with dialogue, debate, dissent, radical imagination, and other features of genuinely democratic culture. Grit does not suggest that learning and self-transformation are involved in engaging with the social context through the educational process to change it. The solution is learned persistence at meaningless and decontextualized lessons. Allegedly teachers can instill grit through rapid-fire behaviorist call-and-response techniques that use hand signals and that resemble animal training regimes.

Grit pedagogy entered the mainstream in 2010 shortly after the global financial crisis and government austerity response. As a form of neoliberal character education, grit puts the burden for economic, academic, and social uplift onto the student and locates academic failure, social maldistribution, in the broken toxically stressed bodies of students.

Meditation Programs

Meditation education programs also express key aspects of resilience. Meditation programs have been popularized in schools. Like grit pedagogy, meditation programs suggest that social contexts create stressors on the student and impediments to learning. Meditation programs presume that students should focus their attention inwardly on the self and away from the broader social world and community. These programs draw on the secular appropriation of Eastern religious traditions and spiritual New Age movements that have expanded since the 1970s and expanded in education since the aughts. For example, the David Lynch Foundation Center for Resilience funds a variety of school programs in transcendental meditation and mindfulness. The foundation website states its mission:

> The David Lynch Foundation helps to prevent and eradicate the all-pervasive epidemic of trauma and toxic stress among at-risk populations through promoting widespread implementation of the evidence-based Transcendental Meditation™ (TM) program in order to improve their health, cognitive capabilities and performance in life.[19]

The subjective turning inward promoted by meditation resilience programs promises students calm minds and better health. But it does not promise to help students understand what and who puts them "at-risk," what broader forces, structures, interests, and ideologies make and reproduce violent and unequal realities that subject youth to "trauma" and "toxic stress."[20] In Chicago, a program called Calm Classroom, started by a former hedge fund manager, contracts with the public district to sell mindfulness meditation programs. Programs involve "breathing, stretching, focusing, and relaxation techniques."[21] Middle school programs include "Mindfulness with Music" that has students listen to music without other distractions. "Mindful Coloring" has students color coloring books and encourages them to focus their attention on coloring. These programs raise several basic questions: about the financial cost to the district (a district in which half of the schools do not have a library and three quarters do not have a librarian), about using classroom time on this as opposed to other activities such as studying subjects or traditions of thought or projects that provide social engagement with their community, about the value of such attention exercises as opposed to, say, exercises that allow students to comprehend how knowledge and learning can be the basis for social and self-understanding, change, and agency. By asking students to turn their focus inward and away from the social world, meditation programs encourage students to comprehend their problems as self-originating rather than socially originating.

Consequently, while the problems facing youth such as poverty and violence are social and require collective action to address, the solutions can only be addressed on the terrain of the self. Meditation school projects actively deny the ways that the self is socially formed by objective forces and realities outside the self and the school. In turn, these projects deny the capacity for students to be subjects whose understanding of social reality and personal experience can be the basis to act with others to change that objective world. These programs translate social and political agency into a form of agency concerned only with self-care, self-therapy, and self-treatment.

As well, resilience programs bolster a broader meritocratic ideology in schools that teaches children to blame themselves for the unequal distribution of life chances. Just as test scores and grades sanctify radically unequal life courses and standards of living under the guise of individual talent and industriousness,[22] resilience pedagogies add affect, behavior, and learned self-control to the pedagogy of self-blame. This is becoming more pronounced as initiatives expand to quantify affect and behavior in schools as "non-cognitive skills" and "objectivize" these behaviors by linking them to quasi-scientific standards from psychology.[23] Similarly, the ubiquitous promotion of "growth mindset" makes affect measurable. Supranational organizations that represent the interests of global corporations spearhead these efforts that aim to bolster the commercialization of behavior and affect through the datafication of hitherto unquantified aspects of everyday life. Once quantified these behaviors then become datafied and run through big data algorithms that further lend them an aura of disinterested objectivity. This quantification translates ideological and political norms imposed by schools (obedience and docility to authority as opposed to questioning authority, for example) into supposedly neutral and disinterested measures.

Play-Based Learning and the Control and Quantification of the Body

The OECD and the World Economic Forum have worked with the world's largest toymaker Lego Group and its philanthropic foundation, Lego Foundation, to promote play-based learning around the world.[24] Lego aims to make play-based learning a quantifiable and measurable learning standard alongside basic skills in math and reading. Nations around the world reform education systems in hopes of raising test scores in order to appear more educationally and economically competitive. Lego aspires to make play itself a legitimate form of education, and the Lego Foundation churns out regular reports and advocacy pieces to make that case.[25]

As well, Lego increasingly integrates their plastic blocks and traditional toys with digital apps and expands their digital education products. Lego stands to profit by making play and the use of their products into education and human development itself. As well, Lego stands to benefit financially as the data collected through the use of their digital products is a form of capital with commercial worth to be traded, used for marketing, run through big data programs or simply hoarded for future use.[26] Supranational organizations such as the OECD, the World Bank, and the World Economic Forum, which represent multinational corporations, see "non-cognitive" skills development, including play-based learning and social and emotional learning, to be an essential part of human capital growth. In this view, investment in non-cognitive human capital skills forms the basis for national and global economic growth.[27] Supranational organizations promote this perspective of non-cognitive skill investment in human capital. As Chandler and Reid point out, supranational organizations, such as the World Bank, that promote the human capital model for development, assume that social and economic problems result from the bad individual capacity for adaptive choice making.[28] That is, these organizations locate the causes of poverty and inequality not within an economic system, capitalism, that prioritizes business owner profit and growth at any cost over human or environmental values. Rather, they frame the causes of social problems as individuals' capacity for making choices to be resilient. Of course, this misrepresents who has and doesn't have social power and how society is organized in systematic ways through, for example, racialized and gendered class hierarchy.

Supranational organizations, corporate philanthropies, and corporations have been promoting play-based learning and the quantification of play-based learning. One corporate philanthropy in particular, the Lego Foundation and the Real Play Coalition of which it is a part have been working with the WEF and the OECD to support the expansion of the measurement, quantification, and assessment of play. The Lego Group, headquartered in Denmark, is the largest toy company in the world, earning nearly $2 billion a year through sales of its plastic interlocking blocks but also its Legoland theme parks, its highly lucrative Hollywood movies and series, and other merchandise. The Lego Foundation, a not-for-profit organization funded by the company, plays a prominent role in promoting play-based learning internationally, promoting the idea of an international educational skills crisis that ought to be met with play-based learning, and encouraging the measurement and assessment of play, the inclusion of such assessment in the OECD Program for International Student Assessment (PISA) international educational comparison tests, and the linkage of quantified play to the United Nations' Millennium Development Goals promoted by the World Bank.[29]

The Lego Group has not been able to rely on a monopoly over the manufacture of plastic bricks. It faces competition from inexpensive Chinese imitators whose bricks fit Legos. For more than a decade, Lego has branched out into merchandising tie-ins, partnering with both DC Comics and Marvel Comics on Lego Super Heroes toys, movies, and video games. They also partner with Pixar on The Incredibles franchise; Disney, Warner Brothers, Universal Pictures on Minions and Minecraft, and many other large media corporations as well.

While to a less extent Lego sells classic sets of bricks without instructions, Lego toys have increasingly moved toward providing premade cinematic and video game narratives for themed toys that interlock corporate branding and merchandising arrangements with their products. Lego sets have concomitantly moved toward instructional kit building with step-by-step instructions for children to build branded toys (DC Comics Batman, Disney scenes, etc.) and moved away from open play. As critics of school commercialism have contended, commercial film franchise tie-ins result in greater prescribed play by children.[30] Critics argue that prescribed play undermines imagination as children are observed imitating and repeating the narratives and ideologies learned from movies or television rather than creating their own narratives.[31] As well, the increase in the sale of instructional kits results in the promotion of rule-following to complete an object of someone else's imagining. This tendency of Lego toys coheres with the Lego Foundation's promotion of instrumental and skills-developing, practical forms of play. Lego toys appear from their website and the Apple App store to be increasingly moving in the direction of the interface of branded toy kits with video game apps. These digital directions for Lego suggest the growing importance for the company of capturing and commercializing the data that children produce through using its products.

The Lego Group actively produces meanings and points of identification in coordination with large media and entertainment conglomerates such as Warner Brothers. The narrative of innocent and authentic creativity, spontaneous imagination, and play coming from the Lego Foundation and their well-funded partners in academia and NGOs sounds quite different from the Lego Group marketing director Michael McNally who celebrated in *The New York Times* the power of Lego movies to sell Legos by getting the film characters/media products inserted into children's play,

> "We know that children's play reality involves mixing and matching characters and backdrops from our classic sets and our licensed properties," Mr. McNally said. "In that way, they can promote any of our mini figures or mini dolls to the role of hero in their own story."[32]

That quote was from 2014 when Lego had just launched the first Lego movie. Currently, Lego Ventures has been spearheading the move of Lego Group into multimedia digital products, seeing education and gaming at the center of product development. Lego Ventures invests in digital content companies with an eye on buying the successful ones.

The quantification of play for the Lego Group has two important dimensions. By inserting play into the global accountability and standards movement spearheaded by supranational organizations OECD and WEF that represent multinational capital, Lego aims to position their business and their products as essential to educational provision, human development, economic growth, and the acquisition of individual skills that contribute to that economic growth.[33] By promoting play as quantifiable, measurable, and integral to global educational comparisons, Lego stands to legitimate itself and its profit-seeking activities in these regards while increasing the likelihood of greater revenue.

If quantified play can be successfully integrated into global comparative educational accountability standards, then play will be measured along with other academic achievements on national tests that form the basis for international comparisons. OECD wields major soft power influence on national policy around the world as nations seek to follow trends and advice to demonstrate global competitiveness and development to other nations. Nationally, efforts will be made to increase test scores by focusing on the skills and dispositions that will be measured. Having successfully lobbied for the incorporation of play-based learning as a measurable skill, Lego will be ready to provide the curriculum materials in the form of Lego products. The Lego Foundation is heavily investing in its work with other organizations to accomplish this legitimation project: Project Zero at Harvard University, collaborations with OECD, WEF, and the Real Play Coalition, to name a few of the most prominent. Second, the agenda for the quantification of play creates the conditions for the increasing convergence of education and media entertainment corporations around digital learning products. This convergence of education and digital media entertainment naturalizes as necessary for learning and human development gamified forms of pedagogy typified in digital SEL apps, biometric measurement systems, personalized learning products, and the interface of physical toys like Legos and drones with digital apps. As well, this convergence creates the conditions for the ever-greater digital measurement and surveillance of children's activity and human activity, the normalization and "making innocent" of total surveillance and commercialization of that surveillance through the discourse of childhood innocence.[34] The social control and commercial extraction/ digital representation possibilities of datafication are part of a broader trend toward the "Internet of Things" (IOT) aiming to integrate the physical world with the internet and digital industry.[35]

The aim of making "resilient" subjects through control of bodies puts the onus for ameliorating the destruction of structural inequality onto the individual student. Such individualizing of responsibility for responding to social violence benefits ruling groups and classes who do not have to give anything up to create the social conditions for economic equality, political power sharing, and cultural institutions structured in deeply democratic ways. More specifically, the new form of corporeal character education allows ruling-class people to evade paying for public education that would give everyone the kind of schools that the richest have and remedy the historical failure to do so. Worse yet, new contracting in the technologies of character formation allows ruling-class people to profit from displacing blame onto others who did not make the conditions that they suffer and endure. The "resilient" student through learned self-control can allegedly be made to withstand the violence of poverty and all of its ancillary effects and withstand symbolic violence that positions them as embodying cultural deficits.

Global Interests and Ideologies of the Targeting of the Body and Affect

The quantification of affect is a global project spearheaded by supranational organizations which represent global corporations that are setting the stage for new forms of digital educational commercialism. The OECD has worked to standardize not just play-based learning but SEL definitions and standards in order to create the conditions for it to be quantified and datafied.[36] In the words of Williamson and Piattoeva, the OECD and the WEF aim to "stabilize the field of knowledge" as a supposed natural science about SEL and create a new policy consensus and common sense about it by drawing together concepts from psychology and economics.[37] Proponents of neoliberal human capital theory are promoting the quantification of SEL.[38] "Non-cognitive skills" like student affect, behavior, and play are purported to be necessary supports for cognitive skills and knowledge acquisition. Williamson and Piattoeva point out that a central aspect of this project involves establishing bounded norms of selfhood in psychological categories.[39]

The objectivizing of SEL is a class and cultural project of ruling groups to secure their hegemony. The elaborate use of positivist ideology in technology is about securing social power as well as cultural dominance. Perhaps the greatest material interest in objectivizing SEL is to translate it into commercially viable data for those who own and invest in educational technology industries.

OECD and WEF reports, websites, and documents show a number of key framing assumptions about the linkage between resilience, SEL, and data manufacture.[40] Among these are: (1) the need for more "private sector involvement" in public education, including public–private partnerships, private financing, and investment.[41] This presumes that technology corporations and banks need to play a greater role in SEL and its quantification; (2) the alignment of human capital (education as a market-based investment that pays off in expanded labor markets, capitalist growth, and global economic competition) with "psycho-informatics" (techniques and technologies that measure, datafy, track, and analyze behavior, affect, and dispositions such as biometric analytic technologies);[42] (3) the need for SEL to be datafied;[43] (4) a view of globalization and technology as the key drivers of change akin to natural forces producing inequality. Such a perspective does not recognize the extent of class antagonism, domination, and hegemonic struggle.[44]

Within this view, individual agency takes shape as resilience, compelled by "forces of nature." Such resilience discourse does not recognize the extent to which particular versions of globalization (global justice movement versus neoliberal globalization) or technology (technology as tool for equality and freedom from domination versus technophilic capitalism) are collective human products, ideological formations that are far from natural or inevitable, and for their propagation require being ongoingly taught and learned; (5) the incitement and commercialization of so-called "soft skills," that is, non-cognitive skills, promoted by SEL as crucial for economic development and the new directions of industry in the "4th Industrial Revolution."[45]

In addition to key framing assumptions, the supranational organizations share certain key constitutive absences that frame their projects. These absences include a tendency to gut educational and social theory and humanities traditions from the discussion of what is needed in schools and society. This may seem contradictory, as the humanities disciplines have historically been thought of as the place where the emotions and senses get developed. Yet, the education of the senses that the humanities has engaged has required interpretation, and interpretation is unassimilable within the quantification and antidialogical behaviorism that most resilience programs mandate. Resilience discourses pair up psychological developmental tropes from empiricist traditions with positivist measures of learning expressed through standardized testing. This produces a particular version of the relationship between individual subjects and knowledge in which individual experiences are valuable in relation to learning only as a means of comprehending the proper dispositions for the consumption of knowledge or comprehending blockages to the efficient consumption of knowledge formed by "bad" habits or trauma.

SEL, play-based learning, meditation, and mindfulness pedagogies draw on empiricist and developmentalist forms of psychology, denying the politics of education, knowledge, and culture. They have to be recognized as a political framing which largely expresses liberal and power-evasive ideologies of education—the impossible claim that knowledge and curriculum are apolitical and must be framed as "neutral"[46]—as universal. Consistent with the denial of the politics of knowledge and curriculum, the World Economic Forum asserts that children should learn to approach problems "the way a computer would."[47] In this view, all problems are technical problems and practical problems, not matters of interpretation and judgment. Such a view presumes that there is no place for critical questions about the relationship between the framing of problems and the interests, ideologies, and social locations of particular groups of people. Yet, the crucial innovation of the latest push for SEL quantification and measurement is its connection to the industry in digital technology contracting, the trade in data, and the continuing growth of impact investing schemes.

In contrast with critical pedagogy, the goal of SEL, play-based learning, grit, and other resilience pedagogies is not to develop in students the capacity to theorize claims to truth, the self, or the social in relation to authority.[48] Critical pedagogy, an educational tradition that emerges from the work among others of Paulo Freire and Henry Giroux and is informed by numerous critical theoretical traditions, aims to engage students in dialogic learning projects that develop critical consciousness for understanding how their experiences are related to the social context and how learning can become a means of collective social engagement. Critical pedagogy, as Giroux suggests, makes learning meaningful to make it critical and socially transformative. It fosters practices that cultivate comprehension of the politics of knowledge, the extent to which the self is socially formed, the contextual dimensions of truth claims, and makes learning central to aspirations for collective forms of self-governance and social agency.[49]

Microschools, UberEd, and Dropout Recovery

Profit and Peril in Resilience to Disaster during Covid-19

The previous chapters provided an overview of how resilience is contributing to digital forms of educational privatization. This chapter illustrates how the long-standing proponents of educational privatization have used the Covid-19 pandemic to justify public funding of for-profit digital technologies in the name of school and district resilience. They have called for expanding school vouchers and scholarship tax credits, both of which exacerbate racial and class inequalities, to fund these schemes.

During the Covid-19 pandemic for-profit cyber microschools and online education brokers, pairing independent teachers with pods, opened for business. Microschools are small private homeschool arrangements typically of neighbors. Cyber education brokers are online businesses that pair parents with would-be instructors who may or may not have teaching experience, teacher training, and certification. Despite the lack of evidence to justify these initiatives, right-wing think tanks called for the expansion of vouchers and scholarship tax credit neovouchers to publicly support these privatization projects as resilience to disaster and school disruption. This chapter details how this episode continues a longer legacy of capitalizing on natural and human-made disaster to promote educational privatization initiatives that could not be accomplished through policy or political means and that have been proven to exacerbate inequality.[1] The chapter situates these developments in terms of broader economic, political, and educational trends. The first section details ongoing natural and human disasters, especially global warming, and the changes that are highly likely to accelerate. The second section covers the ways that privatization proponents used the pandemic to promote vouchers and scholarship tax credit neovouchers to expand microschools and online education brokers that pair independent teachers with parents despite a lack of evidence to justify either the new enterprises or the funding schemes. The third section makes the case that critical and democratic forms of education are a better response to disaster than these education profiteering schemes.

Disaster

Public schools in the United States are now routinely disrupted in significant ways by natural disasters such as hurricanes, severe storms, fires, floods, heat waves, and public health crises that are often caused or exacerbated by global warming.[2] The United States and the world are experiencing these disasters on unprecedented scales and with unprecedented frequency.[3] Climate scientists project these trends to continue even as significant changes to fossil fuel usage may mitigate the extent and extremity of anticipated severe natural conditions.[4] In past decades some of the most high-profile disruptions followed hurricanes Katrina in New Orleans and the Gulf Coast; Irma, Maria, and Harvey in the south; and in Puerto Rico and the U.S. Virgin Islands as well as the California and northwest Pacific wildfires. In their most recent risk assessment report the World Economic Forum projects climate change disruption as the major anticipated social disruption followed by the Covid-19 pandemic.[5] As well, a number of school disruptions are the consequence of human-made disasters, including mass shootings such as at Uvalde, Parkland, and Newtown and the coordinated dismantling of vital public infrastructure such as the coordinated closure of public housing and public schools in urban centers such as Chicago[6] and Detroit.[7] Investors, business people, and rightist ideologues have taken advantage of human-made disaster and natural disaster to advance political and economic agendas, including educational policy aims such as charter and voucher expansion.[8]

Natural disasters are expected to precipitate additional human disasters. In 2002 the US National Security Strategy detailed predictions that as imminent global warming would result in large-scale mass migrations and social upheaval, the role of the US armed forces would become increasingly focused on these social and political upheavals resulting from human-made global warming.[9] Recent scientific studies have found that projections of the effects of global warming are as severe or more severe than previously predicted worst-case scenarios.[10] Scientific studies show that environmental destruction such as deforestation and biodiversity loss through extinction increases the likelihood and severity of global pandemics.[11] As well, there is a shrinking likelihood that an adequate collective response will avert climate "tipping points," beyond which slowing or reversing global warming remains a possibility. For example, as permafrost in Greenland, Antarctica, and the global north melts, it releases vast quantities of methane that significantly increases global warming through the greenhouse effect. The overwhelming global consensus among scientists, the private sector, governments and their disaster relief agencies, and militaries is that disaster and disruption can be anticipated with a very high degree of certainty. While much can and should be done to mitigate the severity of coming disasters and disruptions to schools, there is a widespread scientific and academic consensus that even the most aggressive collective action, such as radically reducing fossil fuels' usage immediately, would not immediately halt the effects of global warming. Consequently, disruptions to schools seen in past years can be expected to not just continue but most likely to increase in frequency.

Capitalizing on Disaster with Resilience

At the outset of the pandemic, leading scholars of educational technology and a leading journal of educational technology counseled caution about a widespread turn to online learning.[12] Yet, most of the United States and much of the world closed schools and rushed to technology-based remote learning, In March 2020 shortly after the declaration of the global pandemic, the first school district in Washington (Bothell) state closed schools and shifted students to technology-based remote learning.[13] By the last week of March, all fifty states had followed suit, and Kansas became the first state to announce the closure of schools for the remainder of the school year. Governors and state education agencies, rather than state legislatures, largely enacted these changes. States that acted later followed the models of states that acted early to close schools, and move to technology-based remote learning. The go-to response in the current pandemic was "distance education" operationalized as virtual schooling (including pods and microschools). In 2020, 82 percent of classrooms used Google Classroom (54 percent) or Canvas (28 percent), and Zoom and Google Meet became the predominant video conferencing apps.[14] Districts across the United States contracted with for-profit technology providers and utilized a variety of online programs.

There were many dire problems accompanying the technology-oriented remote learning approach, including limited plans for special education students, students with disabilities, English language learners, and those predominantly working-class and poor students without access to remote technology.[15] Other problems included inconsistent and incoherent curriculum selection and sequencing and problems with curriculum quality. Students widely reported exhaustion and "zoom fatigue" from long hours on screens. In Chicago, tens of thousands of students signed a petition against online remote learning. Despite the American Academy of Pediatrics recommending a limit of one hour of high-quality daily screen time[16] some districts had elementary-age children in front of screens for seven hours. Youth mental illness and suicide rates increased exponentially.[17] Alternative approaches to the technology-oriented ones, such as outdoor education, were, for the most part, not employed. In part, this owed to the inflexibility faced by administrators and teachers in policy that drove a technology-oriented aspiration to replicate in-person schooling. Consequently, teachers spent inordinate amounts of instructional time devoted to technical problems and spent large amounts of uncompensated time learning to use the technology and setting up online lessons. Technology-oriented remote learning resulted in very high rates of student non-participation, dropout, truancy, and unenrolment. Unequal patterns of student technology use correlated highly with income and class as well as racial inequality.[18] As abundant money flowed to technology companies, alternative ideas about how to keep teachers and immunocompromized personnel and students safe were not developed. There were other possibilities. For example, Sweden never closed K–12 schools during the pandemic but made accommodations for those living in intergenerational households. Swedes considered the much broader social, educational, economic, health, psychological, and cultural costs of school closures and decided that the social costs of school closures outweighed the risks of the disease. While I am not advocating Sweden's approach, it represents an option among others that were not considered.

In the United States, state implementation policy was predominantly a game of follow the leader. Without established policy scholarship guiding the transition, states looked to other states that acted early. As well, certain predominant assumptions were carried forward including the assumption that remote online learning should largely replicate the face-to-face school day. The federal government gave states waivers from assessment requirements and provided bailout funds from the CARE Act. The widespread turn to digital education was facilitated by the tech industry and related players and by the strong relationships between those various players, political leaders, and NGOs.[19]

During the pandemic, think tanks, trade associations, Silicon Valley, venture philanthropists, and certain privatization-oriented politicians promoted online instructional technology as the principal solution to school disruption.[20] Indeed, some technology and privatization boosters at the outset of the pandemic, including New York governor Andrew Cuomo and Bill Gates, both of whom have long histories of promoting public school privatization,[21] took the opportunity to declare the "end of brick and mortar schooling."[22] Cuomo and Gates were not alone in seeking opportunity to take advantage of the disaster to aggressively promote a redistribution of control over schools from communities, the public, educational experts, teachers, and educational leaders to control by large technology companies such as Alphabet (Google), Apple, Microsoft, and educational conglomerates that have been morphing into technology companies such as Pearson, Kaplan, and ETS.[23] Technology companies have long sought to expand their presence in public schooling and the prospects for profit-taking are enormous.[24] Leading test and textbook publishing companies invested millions to lobby for the expansion of test-oriented forms of curricular standardization that resulted in billions of dollars in profit for them.[25] As well, for-profit media companies such as Meta (formerly Facebook) have been involved in the development of adaptive learning software that shifts control of decision-making about curriculum and pedagogy away from teachers and toward technology companies and their corporate foundations such as Chan Zuckerberg Initiative.[26]

Policy think tanks, politicians, and businesspeople have used disaster to promote educational agendas—especially no-bid contracting and privatization in the form of charter expansion and vouchers.[27] Market ideologues and investors have taken advantage of disaster or even sought to use it to create the conditions for profit-seeking in education. This history is pertinent to the current promotion of for-profit technology contracting and educational privatization advocacy during the pandemic as well as advocacy of such contracting as a universal response to disaster and disruption.

School and district closures imposed under the mantle of emergency have been used to achieve previously unachievable policy and political ends such as enacting no-bid contracting for rebuilding and emergency management, dismantling teacher unions, illegally breaking collective bargaining agreements,[28] and implementing previously stifled privatization schemes such as charter school expansion and voucher expansion.[29] One of the most extreme cases of such educational disaster engineering was enacted following Hurricane Katrina in the Gulf Coast.[30] In this case, privatization schemes—including vouchers, radical charter school replacement of entire districts, and for-profit no-bid contracting, the dismantling of the New Orleans public school district and mass firing of the unionized teacher workforce—were enacted, justified under the rubric of emergency and enacted by a junta of business people and corporate consultants. As well, these radical moves had been planned and advocated in advance by pro-privatization ideologues at the Urban Institute and Yankee Institute.[31]

The public sector response has been different from the private sector response. The Federal Emergency Management Agency (FEMA) frames school response to disaster as needing to be less about collectively responding to disaster by supporting educational organizations and more about teaching children and the public to be "resilient to disaster." As a major FEMA report explains, it is about teaching "individuals to assume more responsibility and self-reliance for disaster."[32] Apparently, rather than relying on authoritative government action and expecting fiscal investment in public infrastructure, this report suggests shifting the onus for disaster response to individuals and positions public schools as a key driver of individualized responsibility. This report largely aims to educate students to see disaster as "the new normal" in an increasingly precarious world but, troublingly, to not expect a sufficient public response to it. The only course of action for students within this assumption is to adapt to the new normal rather than collectively act to either avert or mitigate the onset of disaster. Such a resilience logic of individualized responsibility and adaptation may not benefit youth, but it certainly affirms status quo relations of power than benefit financial and political elites and their pursuit of short-term profits.

Technology Isn't the (Only) Solution

After a year of technology-based remote learning during the Covid-19 pandemic, it became clear that technology alone is not the solution. Evidence for the value of a tech solution is weak at best.[33] For policy experts who had followed studies of online education experiments such as for-profit educational management organization K12, Inc's forays into cyber charter schooling and cyber homeschooling, these outcomes were not terribly surprising.[34] New research on the shift to predominantly remote technology finds

> [t]he research evidence…does not support claims that virtual education produces better student outcomes, as compared to conventional face-to-face approaches to teaching and learning in brick-and-mortar schools. In fact, full-time virtual schools, in particular, have yielded very poor outcomes.[35]

The concerns with technology-based remote learning as the default direction for schooling during disruptions have problems that go beyond conventional test-based concerns with efficacy as measured by declines in standardized test scores. Other significant issues include commercial content of the curriculum, concerns about student privacy, and the uses and abuses of collected data, the nature of control over the learning process, the emotional toll on youth, disregard for teacher quality, and willingness to shift teaching to machines.[36] Additional problems include the disregard for student subjectivity and culture, disregard for the social context for learning, disregard for the relationship between learning and student agency, disregard for the cultural politics of knowledge and curriculum,[37] a reduction of the broader purposes and goals of public schooling to narrow, technical, commercial ones, and a reduction of pedagogical approaches to those that accord with transmission models of schooling.[38] Other major problems include "Online exam proctoring software and its biases, unequal access to hardware or internet connectivity, politically-motivated algorithmic grade standardization, and the use of online learning platforms for cheating."[39] Review of research finds

> the use of digital platforms and learning programs is tied to significant threats to the integrity of schools' curriculum and instruction programs, their student assessments, and their data collection and record-keeping practices.[40]

Despite weak evidence for it there was a wholesale rush to implement remote educational technology. Yet, educational profiteers seized on other opportunities during the pandemic as well.

Disruption Response

A variety of options (microschools, education brokers, and dropout recovery services) are being pushed for business reasons, but their value is not supported by evidence. Think tanks such as American Enterprise Institute, Hoover Institution, and Heritage Foundation, which have long advocated disinvestment in traditional public schooling in conjunction with expanding educational privatization, have seized on the pandemic to promote vouchers and scholarship tax credit neovouchers to fund "microschools" or "pods." As the think tank advocacy reports explain, microschool voucher expansion schemes largely coincide with digital privatization as a great number of these microschools are cyber charter and cyber homeschools such as Prenda, and Acton Academies.[41] These think tanks also promote voucher and neovoucher expansion for notable cyber "education brokers" that operate as a kind of "Airbnb for education" or "Uber," connecting parents to instructors for hire. These include Cottage-Class, Friendly Minds, Selected for Families, and SchoolHouse.[42] Micropods and education brokers lack a number of crucial elements and safeguards of public schools, including health, safety, and inclusion standards and oversight for physical school sites, unified standards to assure teacher quality, experienced, licensed, and adequately paid teachers, universal access, adequate administrative support, a steady and reliable funding source, systems for standards and oversight with regard to curriculum and pedagogical approaches, systems, and standards to assure racial, ethnic, linguistic, and ability access, inclusion, and desegregation.

Who Benefits from the Push for a Technology-Centered Response to Disaster?

Three recent advocacy reports have been published advising action based on the preexisting values of the organization. These have been generated by the most powerful right-wing think tanks advocating educational privatization and other market-based reforms such as the erosion of teacher's collective bargaining power and the erosion of quality controls for well-trained and experienced teachers. For example, the American Enterprise Institute published during the pandemic "A Blueprint for Back to School."[43] This report, authored by a who's who of the corporate school reform movement, opens by asserting the primary educational values of a basic skills orientation and the need to relieve workers of parental duty by getting kids back in schools. The blueprint then calls for linking to the Covid-19 disruptions a number of additional long-standing business agenda items that aim to reduce costs at the expense of quality and open the door to unsubstantiated privatization, including: incentivizing the early retirement of the most experienced teachers (getting a younger and cheaper labor force), removing or reducing quality controls over teacher certification and credentials to allow untrained teachers to enter the profession, opening up questions about collective bargaining agreements, and calling for "flexibility" with regard to staffing, labor issues, work hours.[44]

As AEI principally targeted teacher labor, their colleagues at the Heritage Foundation and Hoover Institution seized on a new possibility to promote privatization in the form of "micro pods" or "microschools." Heritage Foundation issued a "backgrounder" titled "Let's Get Small: Microschools, Pandemic Pods, and the Future of Education in America"[45] and Hoover's *Education Next* published an advocacy piece titled "The Rapid Rise of Pandemic Pods."[46] Both pieces celebrate the expansion during Covid-19 of small private schools and businesses, many of which employ cyber schooling. They encourage the withdrawal of students from public schools, the use of pay-for-fee schooling, heavy reliance on dubious cyber schooling, the use of often unlicensed, untrained, and inexperienced teachers as a hopeful development and a model in need of expansion. They write that this model should be expanded through the expansion of vouchers or scholarship tax credits "neovouchers"[47] that induce citizens to redirect their taxes from public schools to private consumption of education. Cyber schooling has a very poor record in terms of traditional measures of academic achievement.[48] Research supports teacher training and licensure that facilitate higher levels of teacher experience.[49] The think tank authors admit that the pay-for-fee model that they promote leads to a lack of school access for poor students. Extolling the virtues of "flexibility" and "quality," the Heritage Foundation piece claims that teachers can earn vastly more in microschools than in traditional public schools.[50] However, a cursory search on a teacher job website indeed.com reveals that chain microschools like Prenda and Action Academies pay teachers near-poverty level wages of $15–20 per hour at Prenda and $30,000–$40,000 per year for lead teacher positions. The Heritage Foundation celebrates the "low barrier to entry" of using people's homes instead of schools and adequate infrastructure that fulfills state standards to serve all students with diverse needs. Both articles focus on how, despite the exclusionary nature of these microschools to the poor who do not have money to pay for these private services, states ought to expand vouchers and neovouchers to subsidize unregulated microschools of questionable quality. This comes despite the research and evidence against vouchers and neovouchers on grounds of exacerbation of racial segregation, erosion of public educational finances, and worsened quality in traditional measures of academic achievement.[51]

The dropout recovery industry has also used the pandemic to vastly expand its for-profit contracting. For example, Graduation Alliance is a for-profit company owned by the large global investment firm KKR. Graduation Alliance got a no-bid contract with New Mexico Education Alliance to hire low-paid telemarketers to follow a script and contact truant youth. These low-paid telemarketers were working for hard-to-get bonuses. In this blurring of public interest and private profit-seeking, two deputy secretaries of education for the state co-authored the Engage New Mexico plan with Graduation Alliance business co-owner and partner Rebekah Richards.[52] The company and Engage New Mexico "had no access to attendance and grade data for the students who got coaching,"[53] which raises serious questions as to the efficacy of the program. Graduation Alliance counted contacts made by these telemarketers rather than actual outcomes as successful interventions.[54] The company made millions despite a lack of credible evidence for its efficacy or success. It then used the white paper co-authored by the owner to tout its activities as proof of success to sell $9 million in contracts with multiple other states, including Arkansas, Michigan, South Carolina, and Ohio.[55] The integration of industry into public policy decision-making, as exemplified in this case, seriously compromises the public interest and public governance.

Despite the lack of research, evidence, or good arguments supporting microschools or pods, these trends are being aggressively advocated by market-based think tanks who see them as an opportunity to advocate the expansion of vouchers and neovoucher scholarship tax credits even as these advocates admit that these schemes are inequitable and exclusionary.[56] This advocacy also comes despite the fact that there is strong research evidence against vouchers and neovouchers in terms of educational quality and equity.[57]

Different Disruptions Demand Different Responses

Different kinds of disruptions may require different kinds of responses. Whereas a public health crisis such as the Covid-19 pandemic might require an extended period of staying home from school, a natural disaster such as hurricane, flood, or wildfire may have the opposite effect, displacing students and staff from their homes. Such displacement from home would likely present dire problems with virtual options as access to hardware and internet would likely be a major obstacle. The response to these varied disasters should not be guided by "market fundamentalist" experiments that in non-emergency times would not succeed politically or as policy. Administrators, legislators, and policymakers should be leery of the opportunistic use of disaster to promote charters, vouchers, neovouchers, digital privatization, and no-bid contracting. The tech tendency in response to disaster has led to an expansion of an antidemocratic transmission model of education.

Tech Response, Learning Loss, and the Problems of the Transmission Model

The seemingly universal, one-sized-fits-all technology response has been promoted and implemented under a particular set of largely private sector assumptions about the social roles and purposes of schooling. The tech sector has been marketing a shift to remote online education for a long time. During the pandemic this marketing shifted to justifying the tech central approach as a response to the disaster and disruption. Historically, this set of assumptions about knowledge as something that is to be delivered has been referred to as "transmission models of schooling" and sometimes also referred to as "banking education."[58] In this view, knowledge is positioned as an object or commodity to be produced by teachers and consumed by students. There is a long legacy of business groups promoting this version of schooling and emphasizing perceived values for the future workplace of working-class students such as most paramount basic skills and submission to authority.[59] The technology-heavy response has also bolstered the conjunction of market fundamentalism, "solutionism," "innovation," and techno-utopianism that positions technology as inherently beneficial and a propellant for economic development and opportunity.[60] Remote learning through technology lends itself to the transmissional model of pedagogy and a standardized curriculum.

The Value of Data

Ben Williamson and Jathan Sadowski explain why the new business of educational data and virtual approaches tend toward standardization and the transmission model. As Sadowski details, the capture of data from student behavior is a kind of financial capital with exchange value. Due to the possibilities of Big Data, data accumulation from students is seen as potentially financially lucrative in the future even if in the present there are no direct uses for the data.[61] Moreover, as Williamson's research shows, supranational organizations such as the OECD and

World Economic Forum are attempting to construct a "science" of social emotional learning and are promoting the standardization of measurement of social emotional learning through data surveillance, data accumulation, and data analysis.[62] That is, the tech tendency tends to promote approaches to teaching and learning that disregard individual student and teacher uniqueness, cultural differences, the social context for learning, and the ways that these differences are crucial to the meaning of and motivation toward what is learned.[63] The tech tendency and the transmission model it promotes run contrary to democratic values for social understanding as the basis of civic participation, learning as the basis for shared agency, and dispositions for dialogue, debate, dissent, curiosity, and creativity that are the lifeblood of democratic societies.

The digital privatization trend and technology contracting expanded during the Covid-19 lockdowns tend to promote the transmissional model of schooling and assumptions of human capital/banking education. Adaptive learning technology, biometric analytic pedagogy, the implementation of artificial intelligence digital avatars for language arts, and the technology integration with social emotional learning[64] exemplify the growing trend of capturing student behavior and translating it into commercially valuable data.[65] These technologies tend to rely upon frequent testing and teaching to tests, reducing learning to that which can be quantified and measured. New technologies such as these continue the legacy of transmissional models of schooling.

The Language of Learning Loss

The discourse of "learning loss" during Covid-19 has presumed a standardized body of knowledge that ought to be transmitted and consumed by students based in appropriate grade level and presumed developmental stage. Scholars such as David Berliner and Lori Shepperd have questioned the underlying assumptions about fixed bodies of knowledge that supposedly have to be mastered by students on a rigid timeline.[66] As these scholars point out, the value on aggregated annual progress on discreet subjects of study is a social construct rather than a fixed natural reality or need. Moreover, the construct of learning loss has been promoted by the ed-tech and testing industries as a problem that outsourcing of their products solves.[67] The assumption of aggregated learning also actively denies that knowledge is always implicated in cultural politics and power relations. That is, different classes and cultural groups produce knowledge and knowledge expresses the material and symbolic interests of classes and groups vying for social dominance. As Antonio Gramsci explains, the dominant bloc tends to universalize its own knowledge as neutral, common sense, and beyond contestation while representing the knowledge of less powerful groups and classes as less legitimate and partisan.[68] This universalization of particular class and cultural knowledge appears in journalism in the guise of disinterested objectivity. Knowledge, made by particular people with particular social, cultural, and class positions, ideologies, and interests, is rendered as neutral, disinterested, and beyond dispute. As well, the processes of standardized testing deny the possibility of students to question, debate, and engage in dialogue with those making the truth claims on the tests. Such dialogic exchange denied by standardized testing is in a form that approximates democratic social relations much more than does the top-down, hierarchical social relations fostered by the transmission model.

The transmission model misunderstands the process of learning and knowledge creation which are based in dialogue and exchange rather than the depositing of knowledge from one person into another.[69] Instead, democratic and critical approaches to education emphasize the co-creation of knowledge through dialogue, the relationship between claims to truth and the social locations, values, and assumptions of students and teachers. This public, civic, and democratic approach values dialogue, debate, curiosity, creativity, and a central concern for motivation driven not by threats and fear, behaviorism and constant testing but interest in self, society, and culture. Response to disruption should be guided by some overarching principles that accord with the broader public and democratic purposes and roles of public schooling.

Some of these principles include flexibility to changing contexts; context-specific curriculum and pedagogy; meaningful learning that relates student experience to the disaster/disruption as well as the broader context and provides the tools to interpret and understand the social causes of what is individually experienced; positioning knowledge and learning as tools to comprehend and potentially act on the situation with others; providing tools of interpretation to comprehend how different classes and cultural groups might be disparately impacted by disaster.

From Resilient to Democratic Adaptation to Disruption

Public schools play an important role in democratic societies of preparing students with skills and know-how not only for participation in the economy but also for participation in collective self-governance and civic participation. Public schools participate in producing forms of selfhood and visions of the future of society. The public role of public schools requires approaches to pedagogy and curriculum as well as school organization and design that both model democracy and create the conditions for democracy throughout society. When addressing how public schools serve the public, it is crucial to consider the greatest public problems facing the United States and the world (such as capitalism's exploitation of nature, people, and the public sphere, global warming, nuclear threat, worsening inequality, and democracy threatened by rising totalitarianism and money in politics) and the ways that these different educational approaches foster capacities of students and the public to respond.[70]

Democratic approaches to schooling are culturally meaningful and relevant, engaging student experience and culture that relate learning to the social context and that create the conditions for student agency.[71] To develop the capacity to participate as a citizen requires knowledge and skills of not just subjects and content but dispositions for interpretation, judgment, dialogue, debate, dissent, and habits of curiosity. Democratic schooling fosters the capacity to comprehend claims to truth in relation to the social authority of the claimant and to develop a sense of self-reflection about how one's assumptions, values, and social position inform one's interpretations.[72] Scholarship on democratic education provides guidance for responding to disaster and disruption in ways that further the public roles and purposes of public schooling, model democracy, and foster knowledge, skills, and dispositions for democratic social relationships and institutions across society.

Different approaches to responding to disruption can facilitate these public educational values. For example, during the Covid-19 pandemic when it was widely believed that in-person schooling indoors could be dangerous for children, there were a number of options for how schools, teachers, and students could transform a limitation into an opportunity. During Covid-19 policy could have promoted a shift to schooling outdoors, to break with standards-based measures of academic achievement and wholly embrace the tenets described above: make the natural and built environment the basis for learning about the locale, geography, natural science, the history of place, engage with public problems observed in the locale, use the specificity of local context as the basis for learning traditional subject matter such as mathematics, social science, language arts, science. As well, a turn to the locale could have enabled an opportunity to investigate how student experience is informed by the broader social context and, as well, could have enabled an opportunity to make learning the basis for acts of social change and social intervention about pressing matters of public import. Such an engagement with place and experience and with making learning meaningful, critical, and socially transformative would be tremendously motivating to students.[73] Instead, during the pandemic, schools turned in the opposite direction to standardized, homogenous, decontextualized online programs, and canned curricula.

Consider how contemporary extreme storms and climate conditions, flooding, and wildfires are increasingly understood as the result of global warming. The affected geography itself can be the basis for curriculum about the science of geological, climate, environmental, and human-produced change. The historical forces and structures that produced the reality experienced by students can be studied, including the natural history predating human activity, the history of Anthropocene industrialization, the development of capitalism, the role and science of technological developments in the production of human-made global warming, the cultural and political forces, interests, and structures at play in addressing or refusing to address the problem and the ways that these realities are impacting the present and the community. Curriculum can then build on the analysis and understanding of what produced the experience of the present by learning to imagine a variety of responses to these lived conditions: What kinds of social, political, ethical, ecological, economic, and technological actions and innovations can address the public problem? Such centering of the public problem and lived experience in relation to the learning of traditional subjects can make learning meaningful, socially engaged, and potentially socially transformative.

The first three chapters have offered a historical and more recent account of the rise of resilience discourse in education and the extents to which it is imbricated with material and symbolic interests and the expansion of digital educational privatization. The next chapter develops this account by illustrating how key players in the corporate school reform movement, venture philanthropists, who have long been proponents of neoliberal educational restructuring, have been some of the most significant figures to use resilience for digital educational privatization.

From Venture Philanthropy to Digital Privatization—New Schools Venture Fund, Leap Innovations, and the Selling of Digital Student Resilience

For decades, a particular version of philanthropy—venture philanthropy—has played an outsized role in promoting educational privatization and corporatization. This chapter details how some of the key figures and organizations involved in the venture philanthropy project of neoliberal privatization of education transitioned to digital educational privatization. They have done so in large part by replacing overt market-based rhetoric with resilience language and concepts and by making resilience the content of their digital educational products. This chapter considers the cases of two venture philanthropists that have become prominent purveyors of digital educational privatization: the New Schools Venture Fund and Leap Innovations.

The New Schools Venture Fund (NSVF) is a nonprofit venture philanthropist that aims to support and finance for-profit and market-oriented education initiatives. As a funding arm that worked with large venture philanthropists such as the Bill and Melinda Gates Foundation and local venture philanthropies such as Chicago Renaissance 2010 (a neoliberal educational restructuring plan spearheaded by the Commercial Club of Chicago), the New Schools Venture Fund was a central player in venture philanthropy supported charter school expansion. NSVF has increasingly moved toward funding for-profit education digital start-up companies for which resilience forms the content—products such as Class Dojo, Amira Learning, and Centervention among many others. Similarly, Phyllis Lockett, the head of Chicago's corporate school reform plan Renaissance 2010, started a company called Leap Innovations to expand adaptive learning technology. Although I am pointing out the development of digital privatization from earlier forms of educational privatization, educational privatization in the form of charters and vouchers has continued to increase.[1] At the same time new insidious forms of educational privatization are being rolled out. NSVF and Leap Innovations exemplify the expansion of educational privatization from for-profit management of schools to digital contracting for curriculum and pedagogy. This chapter examines this expansion that Couldry and Mejias refer to as "the colonization of the lifeworld"[2] and details how resilience concepts such as social emotional learning are at the center of digital privatization becoming the content of apps and platforms. The first section provides a background on the rise of venture philanthropy in education and explains the shift toward digital privatization. The second section examines some digital projects and products of NSVF and their use of resilience concepts. The third section considers the use of resilience concepts of Leap Innovations to promote their personalized learning platform and their misappropriation of critical and progressive language.

Venture Philanthropy

Venture philanthropy, which began in the early 1990s, reimagined charity through the neoliberal lens and language of business. Venture philanthropist organizations, though nonprofits, describe their giving as "investments," aim for "return on investment," and seek to "scale up" and "leverage" school models. Venture philanthropists broke with long-standing giving trends dating back to the beginnings of modern philanthropy known as "scientific philanthropy" that largely developed out of Andrew Carnegie's advocacy as found in his book *The Gospel of Wealth*. Venture philanthropists direct the use of the money they give, retaining control over funding and using funding to influence and control public priorities and public policy. Large venture philanthropists in education include the Bill and Melinda Gates Foundation, the Eli and Edyth Broad Foundation, the Walton Family Foundation, and the Michael and Susan Dell Foundation.

The large venture philanthropists in the United States focused on different signature neoliberal educational restructuring projects. Gates, most notably, promoted the expansion of privately managed charter schools. Broad promoted the privatization of teacher education and leadership preparation programs and database tracking projects. Walton, most notably, pushed voucher schemes. Venture philanthropists organized their giving so that grantees would compete with one another for scarce funds to achieve the priorities of the grantor. For example, Gates dangled millions of dollars to states to induce them to design the most aggressive plans to lift caps (restrictions) on the number of charter schools allowed by the state. After most states complied in hopes of winning funding, only a couple of states per year received money. Staff at the venture philanthropies brought this approach into the Obama Department of Education for his signature education program, Race to the Top.

Despite being nonprofit foundations, venture philanthropists have aggressively expanded the privatization and corporatization of K–12 education, teacher education, and educational leadership. They have promoted private management and private ownership of public schools and the expansion of managerialism and corporate culture in administration and school design while emphasizing the economic roles and purposes of public schools in making students into workers and consumers above all else as opposed to engaged citizens capable of collective self-governance. Despite spending hundreds of millions of dollars influencing public policy, there has been little to show in terms of benefits on the terms of the proponents of these market-style reforms. Standardized test scores have been largely on par with traditional public schools. However, there have been a number of social costs of these various privatization schemes.[3] Chartering has worsened racial segregation and caused disciplinary push-out of students with learning needs; special education and English Language Learner students have also been pushed out from charters.[4] Chartering has resulted in lower teacher pay, union busting, and the expansion of a less educated and less experienced teacher workforce.[5] As well, chartering has fostered vast real estate investment profiteering in which real estate investors create charter schools, get free or cheap real estate from districts, and then lease the use of the school building back to the district.[6] The public pays twice for the school building all to enrich an already rich investor.[7] In addition, venture philanthropy has allowed superrich individuals and corporate foundations to usurp public governance over educational priorities, thereby facilitating a "de-democratization" of public education. The public gives tax breaks to billionaires that allow the billionaire to influence and steer educational policy and practice in line with their perspectives and interests. The teacher bashing that characterized the corporate school reform movement led by venture philanthropists and the endless red tape for teachers in the name of "accountability" and "standards" have resulted in a teacher shortage.

Venture philanthropy has its large players such as the big three that fund more local venture philanthropy organizations. In the United States, between 2006 and 2018, venture philanthropists gave half a billion dollars to charter school promoting associations at the state level.[8] Venture philanthropists built a bureaucratic infrastructure for the nonprofit organizations, promoting profiteering in education. For example, millions also went to the Illinois Network of Charter Schools and New Schools for Chicago that promoted charter expansion in the state and city.[9] In Chicago the Gates Foundation funded the Commercial Club of Chicago Civic Committee's project Renaissance 2010 which was a project to close traditional public schools and replace them with ununionized charter schools. Renaissance 2010 was managed by a businesswoman named Phyllis Lockett. Gates also funded the New Schools Venture Fund that acted as a financing organization for charter expansion. NSVF was created by a billionaire venture capitalist named John Doerr. Lockett would go on to create a digital education company called Leap Innovations that sells personalized learning programs and for which resilience concepts are at the center.

The two key drivers of educational privatization are profit and ideology. These venture philanthropists moved into digital technology in education as for-profit contracting was expanding to new highs. Nearly all US schools closed in the spring of 2020, with the majority turning to a small number of remote learning apps such as Google Classroom and a variety of commercial apps. During the pandemic, Google Classroom jumped from 40 million to 150 million users globally, and Zoom was used by 125,000 schools in twenty-five countries.[10] Prior to the Covid-19 pandemic, new technologies were among the new frontier of commercial opportunities in contracting with public schools. The pandemic vastly expanded the global use of online teaching platforms.

Ideologically, the corporate school reform movement peaked around 2010 with overt celebration of privatization and corporate models of reform and the allegedly hard discipline of business-style accountability. Venture philanthropy represented the neoliberal ideological agenda of celebrating all things private and denigrating public goods and services, centering the metaphors of consumer choice and business competition in education, and framing public schools as primarily preparing future workers and consumers. The financial crisis of 2008 put a dent in the neoliberal idealization of business as the model for all social problems. For example, for the first time, surveys showed support for socialism in the United States reaching unprecedented highs. A number of business-style educational leaders who had been nationally celebrated for their brutal disciplinary tactics, such as Michelle Rhee in D.C. and Rod Paige in Houston, were discovered to have committed fraud by reporting miraculous standardized test score improvements. The alleged objectivism and depersonalization of the metrics promoted by the standards and accountability movement appeared to many to be inhumane and disconnected from questions of student culture and identity. Parents and students began questioning the value of standardized testing, and studies showed the racism and classism inherent in tests. Activists organized standardized test refusal such as the opt out movement, and many linked the rejection of standardized testing to the broader corporate reform model and the even broader problems with privatization of public good and services, exacerbating inequality.

As well, public attention to the problems with venture philanthropy began to become more mainstream around 2010. Former Republican assistant secretary of education and advocate of privatization turned liberal defender of public schooling Diane Ravitch described the venture philanthropists as "billionaire boys clubs." While Ravitch was right that venture philanthropy represents a usurping of educational governance by an economic super-elite, the liberal criticism failed to comprehend how venture philanthropy is part of a broader racialized class-based struggle over public goods and services that is global, how venture philanthropy represents a struggle of public versus privatized governance, and how it needs to be comprehended in terms of the cultural politics of knowledge, curriculum, and pedagogy. A major player in venture philanthropy in education has been the New Schools Venture Fund.

New Schools Venture Fund—Resilience as Digital Product

The New Schools Venture Fund was created by John Doerr and business partner Brook Byers. Venture philanthropist Eli Broad devised a plan to create a "revolving fund to build charter school facilities."[11] Broad initially funded NSVF with over $10 million to invest in charter school facilities, and the returns would fund the expansion of future charter school startups. Businesswoman Kim Smith, who helped Wendy Kopp start Teach for America, designed NSVF and served as the first CEO. Teach for America has been criticized for undermining teacher certification and teacher unions and being a mill that replaces experienced certified teachers with low-skilled, low-paid first-time teachers who typically last no longer than three years and most often transition into business. Doerr and Bill Gates were the earliest investors in NSVF.[12] NSVF was supposed to provide not just start-up capital but management advising for charter boards. Such advising was intended to provide "accountability" as many early charter schools failed. Such a concept of accountability through management support runs counter to the idealization of competition and choice, resulting in weak charter models being allowed to "fail" and "go out of business," as typified in a central ideal of business accountability animating the charter movement.

Early on Doerr was quite explicit about his beliefs in the inherent efficiencies of private sector markets and his animosity toward public education going so far as describing public education as "arguably the largest or second largest most screwed up part of our economy."[13] Public education, he inexplicably stated, "kills about 2 million kids in the country every year."[14]

NSVF built on its charter start-up and advising educational "innovation" activities to fund for-profit and nonprofit educational technology businesses. More recently NSVF added "diversifying leadership" after years of criticism of the racism of the charter movement for having worsened racial segregation, engaged in racialized disciplinary practices against working-class and poor students of color, and engaged in push-outs of special education students who are disproportionately non-white. The diversification of school leaders does not address the racial inequality produced by the charter movement, nor does it address NSVF's complicity in it as a major funder and promoter of charter expansion.

Following the major role in charter expansion in the United States, Doerr and colleagues would go on to expand NSVF to fund for-profit educational technology start-up companies and nonprofits. New School Venture Fund lists 117 educational technology ventures on their website. Forty-three businesses that NSVF funds or has funded are for-profit social emotional learning companies that sell services in resilience. These companies include Class Dojo, Centervention, and Amira Learning. I briefly examine these three for-profit digital education companies trading in resilience.

Class Dojo

Class Dojo is a for-profit classroom management program that runs as
an app on smart phones. It is in 80 percent of US schools overall and
95 percent of K–8 schools. It uses behaviorism to levy disciplinary
practices for surveillance on children while inducing them to generate
commercially valuable data.[15] The company uses the data it collects from
providing its program for free in schools to market lucrative pay-for-fee
at-home programs in mindfulness, growth mindset, and other resilience
content. The resilience content in the school such as the program
"Mindful Breathing with Mojo" can be shared with parents to promote
parental purchases of similar resilience products. Mojo is a green
animated character shaped like a condom that wears a karate headband in
accordance with the martial arts-themed name of the product. "Mindful
Breathing with Mojo" involves students in watching a video that has
students focus on their breathing and then watch a red balloon rise that
carries a box. The video instructs students to put their problems in the
box and watch it float away into the sky. Following the video students are
asked two questions: "How do you feel after taking time to breathe?" and
"When could you use breathing to help you tame your beast?" The last
slide directs students to share this lesson with parents and has a link.[16]

On one level, this little lesson reveals the banality of the mindfulness
curriculum. Students are already quite aware that they breathe. They
surely notice the changes in their own breathing in other aspects of
schooling such as gym class and music instruction and that attention
to breathing has a purpose related to developing a skill. The time spent
focusing on breathing is presumed to reduce anger and produce a state
of docility as evidenced by the leading question about "taming one's
beast." The aim to focus students on themselves and their own bodily
functions is linked by the video to a prescription to ignore or deny
problems that the students experience and that may cause them to feel
stress, anger, or other unpleasant emotions. The goal is to ignore the
problems and make the emotions dissipate by turning attention inward
to the body itself, to focus on the present not the past.

Why not rather make the feelings that students have and the problems that generate those feelings objects of focus, discussion, and the basis for investigation? Such investigation into the problems student experience and the feelings those problems foster can be the basis for socially situated self-understanding. Moreover, such social and self-understanding could be the basis for students to act on the very problems that are troubling them in the first place. For example, in an urban school district composed principally of Black and Brown students, critical mathematics lessons in fraction, decimals, and percentages can engage students in analyzing experiences of racial profiling by police. Learning the mathematical concepts in this case becomes a tool to comprehend disparate treatment and racialized class violence. It can also form the beginning of projects to intervene socially and politically to collectively challenge the experience. Such critical pedagogical projects make learning meaningful but also contribute to translating feelings of powerless, hopelessness, and despair about knowledge and schooling into feelings of capacity, hope, and agency to use knowledge for social and self-understanding and public impact. In contrast, mindfulness programs such as Class Dojo's aim not to help students comprehend the emotions that they experience and the forces that produce those emotions. Rather, they aim to pacify students by turning their attention away from the social and emotion. There is a politics to opting for such pacification in favor of critical curriculum and critical pedagogical practice. The freeware that is now ubiquitous in US schools is a foot in the door for highly lucrative commercialism.

Centervention

Centervention's Zoo U is a computer application that was developed with funding from New Schools Venture Fund. It teaches students social and emotional learning by having them sit in front of a computer screen instead of interacting with human beings. Students watch animated cartoons and play video games about social interactions. The owners promote the program stating, "Every student enters your classroom with unique life experiences, interests and abilities. Why not meet their individual needs with social emotional learning tailored to their specific strengths and weaknesses?"

Promises of attention to student experiences and interests come despite the fact that the technology is incapable of engaging with the unique specificities of student subjectivity or cultural context. Centervention has four animated games based on grade-level K–middle school. The first two are zoo games. One is a superhero game. One is an island game. The fifth is a story-making game for students with autism.[17] Zoo Academy for grades K–1 has students create an avatar in the game. They play a series of eighteen scenes by making choices about how to communicate with other characters. Students choose dialogue and tone.

> Throughout the game, students will help animals like Owlivia the owl learn to respect others' personal space and not call out in class, and Tango the gorilla, who needs some pointers on making new friends. While assisting their classmates inside of the online program, students will learn and practice these skills themselves. For example, in scene 14, it's Mariana's (a game character) birthday and there's a party at school with cupcakes. The player and other students hear Mariana talking about her party that will happen outside of school over the weekend. The player will need to use **coping strategies** and **emotion regulation** to deal with the disappointment/hurt/anger of not being invited to the out-of-school party.

The students' use of the game is recorded, and their social and emotional skills are quantified on a dashboard for the teacher. If a student selects what is deemed to be the wrong affect, behavior, or tone choice, the teacher gives the student the scene to repeat until they are clear about the acceptable course of action and tone for the characters. The evaluated social and emotional skills are communication, cooperation, emotion regulation, empathy, impulse control, and social initiation.

Part of what is concerning about this program is that particular behavioral, affective, and tone values and norms are prescribed for students in ways that are universalized regardless of social context, class difference, and cultural and ideological difference. The primary values promoted by the program are learned self-regulation, obedience to authority, and accepting a pedagogical arrangement that is hierarchical rather than dialogic and exchange oriented. In some contexts, the values that are made universal norms are at odds with educational values or values for democracy and justice. Sometimes these dispositions are a liability. For example, emotion regulation and impulse control can be beneficial values when exercising discipline in the pursuit of learning a skill. However, these same dispositions may be a liability when it comes to participating in collective forms of self-governance in schools or society in pursuit of democratic community and social relationships. As French philosopher Jean Luc Nancy pointed out, anger is a political sentiment.[18] Outrage at injustice and indignance at forms of control antithetical to human freedom are not only a part of a wide range of human emotions but are forms of emotion essential to ethical, political, and just resistance and reaction to oppressive social situations and forces.

Similarly, communication and cooperation can be valuable in some contexts but in other contexts of power imbalance, communication and cooperation can be the basis for participation with or collaboration with oppression and injustice. Because these dispositions are taken up in depoliticized and decontextualized ways, they do not deepen students' understandings of social and emotional skills. This is not an abstract issue. The states of Texas and Florida, for example, have required teachers to teach history with "intellectual diversity" or ideological "balance," aiming to represent right-wing views in the classroom. A notable outcome of this was a school principal in Texas requiring teachers to teach "both sides of the holocaust." Another law in Florida has banned teachers from suggesting that any one race should be made to feel guilt or shame for historical violence against others. Slavery, for example, should not be taught as a systematic historical violence committed by one racial group, namely, white people against Blacks. In this example, Republican legislators in the state of Florida make ethical historical responsibility into a guilty emotion that ought to be refused because it "harms" white students. Rather than addressing the ethical and political values at stake in this example, Republican politicians have shifted the debate onto the terrain of feelings, affect, and the comfort of students. All students ought to learn about slavery: who benefited from it, who was killed and injured by it, why it existed, how it fit into the society of that day, why it was wrong, and how the ethical and political insights gleaned can inform today's aspirations for democracy, equality, and freedom.

What would be preferable to socially and politically decontextualized behavioral skills being taught would be dispositions that accord with democratic social relationships and intellectual habits of engaged citizenry. The former involves skills and dispositions for curiosity, debate, dialogue, dissent. The latter involves the intellectual tools to interpret and comprehend experience and the self as socially formed, to translate individual problems into public problems, and to develop a sense of agency in which learning becomes a means of understanding and addressing public problems through shared projects.

Amira Learning

NSVF invested in ed-tech start-up Amira Learning, which is another for-profit company that contracts with schools. Amira Learning's avatar teaches K–3 students reading by having students sound out words, but it offers nothing in the way of engaging with the meaning of language or the social meaning of texts. Learning in these examples is about nothing more than the learning of discrete and decontextualized knowledge and technical skills, rather than understanding that could form the basis for social comprehension and action. One Amira lesson, *Duck Is Stuck*, illustrates this by repeating a long legacy of nearly nonsensical phonics-oriented stories:

> Duck is stuck in the muck. A pup can tug on the Duck. But Duck is stuck. A cub can tug on Duck. But Duck is stuck. The sun is out. What luck! No mud. No muck. Duck is not stuck.[19]

Aside from teaching ungrammatical sentences, it has little to offer as a story that relates to something that students can find motivating, meaningful, or socially engaged. These standardized texts, despite being packaged as assuring literacy through advanced technology, harken back to the 1950s and the widespread implementation of phonics-oriented basal "Dick and Jane" readers. Contrast it with a couple of board books by Doreen Cronin: *Click, Clack Moo: Cows That Type* or *Duck for President*. The former early reading book tells a story about Farmer Brown's animals going on strike over conditions at the farm and writing demand letters to Farmer Brown to improve conditions. The latter tells the story of Farmer Brown's animals questioning his rule and running a political election to replace his governance. Unlike the Amira lesson, these books teach similar language yet offer entertaining narratives with social concepts that can be engaged with varying degrees of complexity. These books offer narratives that make language learning centrally about questioning social authority and recognizing social conflicts and solidarity. However, to engage with the questions that the books raise demands dialogue between teachers and students, something decidedly impossible with this technology.

Amira Learning raises an obvious question as to the implications of putting children in front of a computer instead of a human being. Strictly in terms of technical efficacy, studies have shown that human instruction in reading is more effective than screen-based instruction.[20] Amira Learning purports to be engaged in "social and emotional learning." Founder Mark Angel was asked about social and emotional learning by *Forbes*:

> an employee told us not to underestimate the emotional issues associated with putting an avatar in front of any person, much less a child. We've been learning how truthful and powerful that observation is ever since. The whole force and magic of one-to-one tutoring is the dialogue that happens between the mentor and the learner. That dialogue is intensely emotional for the learner and involves a lot of dependence, trust and interaction. We've come to believe that every learning experience is deeply social and emotional, and we must

understand those elements as we're creating this interaction between technology, students and teachers."

In this case "social and emotional learning" appears to be simply empty rhetoric as the platform does not engage students in socially engaged pedagogy, contribute to their understanding of human emotions or their own emotions, or allow for dialogue. While Amira touts its capacity for differentiated instruction by being able to have an adjustable pace for its canned content, it does not in any way engage with student differences with regard to culture, language, experience, identity, or class position. Such engagement would require human instruction that relates knowledge, learning, and narratives to both students' experiences and the broader social context—capacities the technology does not have.

Resilience as Digital Product II: Leap Innovations

Phyliss Lockett headed Chicago's Renaissance Schools Fund, which was the funding arm of the Commercial Club of Chicago's Renaissance 2010 plan for Chicago Public Schools. The Commercial Club is a century-old organization that promotes the agendas of the largest corporations in the city. Renaissance 2010 was a privatization plan to close neighborhood public schools and replace them with an array of privatized charter schools with private management.[22] Some of these schools subcontracted management from nonprofit charter management organizations to for-profit management companies like Edison Learning. These for-profits make money by reducing expenses and pocketing the difference between tax revenues and expenditures. Renaissance 2010 was implemented by Mayors Daley and later Emanuel and was launched by future Obama secretary of education Arne Duncan, who aggressively promoted corporate school reform and neoliberal educational restructuring. Like Duncan, Lockett frequently described applying business models of education reform as a "social justice" agenda and education as the "civil rights issue of our day." The consequences of Lockett's work hardly look like "social justice." Consequences include the replacement of public schools with privatized charters: no improvement or worse standardized test performance, de-unionizing the teacher workforce, worsening racial segregation, and increasing administrator pay and decreasing teacher pay, disciplinary push-out of harder to educate students with special education and language acquisition needs.[23] As well, these charters were involved in de-democratizing community control by getting rid of the democratically elected local school councils. Chartering in Chicago resulted in a shift in governance away from teachers and communities, and it concentrated governance power in the hands of unelected charter boards and administrators. Chartering as spearheaded by Lockett and the Commercial Club was also involved in the business-led plan to raze the ten large public housing sites in the city and close the neighborhood schools in those communities as part of the dispossession of people from their homes.

Renaissance 2010 and the Renaissance Schools Fund represent a particular dimension of the educational privatization agenda. The venture philanthropists use nonprofit organizations to bolster the expansion of for-profit education companies that seek to transform public education into a private industry in large part through contracting and school management. The turn of the venture philanthropists toward digital privatization represents a new direction for the privatization agenda even as chartering, vouchers, and tax scholarship neovouchering continue. Digital privatization also seeks to expand profit-seeking through contracting, but it takes privatization in altogether new directions characterized by the quantification, datafication, and commercialization of student subjectivity. NSVF and Leap exemplify this shift in educational privatization that uses resilience concepts to quantify behavior and affect and make selfhood itself into a commodity for investment and profit.

Leap Innovation's primary project is Personalized Learning in digital form. Leap justifies what they do through resilience concepts such as the need for "mindfulness" and "growth mindset" and "cultural competencies" in the service of neoliberal values of schooling for workforce preparation and teaching as data management. For example, Lockett states in an interview that the "next big step" for personalized learning is, "We really need to upskill and reskill our educator workforce. Educators not using a Learning Management System— that's nonnegotiable, especially in the context that we are preparing students for a digital economy."[24] Invoking techophilic tropes, Lockett's rhetoric suggests that the need for the digital surveillance of teachers is somehow justified by the claim that schooling prepares the future digital workforce.

If Lockett were correct that the future of work for most students involves the symbolic manipulation of data and programming, that work would require analytic and interpretation skills. However, there is no sense of how Leap fosters modes of pedagogy other than a transmission model of pedagogy. Furthermore, studies have shown that programming and other digital work represents a small amount of the labor force of the future. What is projected for the future is the growth of service labor.[25] The digital future of labor, even if this were a correct prediction, would not justify teaching with a "learning management system" as opposed to teaching through dialogue. In fact, the pandemic demonstrated the disastrous results of shifting entire school populations onto learning management systems, at all levels of K-12 but particularly at the early grades. Not only did this result in massive student dropping out, health problems such as headaches, and emotional problems, but it hit hardest working-class and poor and Black and Brown students who rejected or were unable to access these technologies at extremely high rates. What Lockett calls "upskilling" and "reskilling" the teacher workforce represents, rather, teacher "deskilling" as technology displaces teacher decision-making about curriculum and pedagogy while preventing critical forms of teaching that engage with students' experiences, cultures, and social contexts for learning.

Leap Innovations received major funding from the Chan Zuckerberg Initiative. In 2018 CZI gave a $14 million grant to Leap "to bring personalized learning programs into more Chicago schools."[26] CZI is a leading philanthrocapitalist organization whose Summit program also aims to promote digital Personalized Learning. CZI is organized as a limited liability corporation that includes both for-profit and nonprofit businesses. It is able to move money and data around within the company between these businesses, and, because it is an LLC, its workings remain secret and beyond public oversight and accountability. In Chicago alone Leap Innovations scored about $6.5 million in contracts to run pilot studies and do professional development to shift student eyeballs from teachers to screens.[27]

Framed as being about equity, Leap Innovations appropriates critical and progressive language including terms such as "agency," "praxis," and "culturally relevant." However, Lockett redefines these terms to transform their meanings to be opposed to their origins and their social justice aspirations. She instead redefines them through values of vocationalism and instrumentalism: school to work. "What is personalized learning? Personalized learning is FOCUSED on, LED with and DEMONSTRATED by the learner, and is CONNECTED to career-relevant, real-world skills and opportunities." The Leap website features a quote from Lockett in which agency is defined not by developing the capacity to take political and social action but rather to have consumer choice in learning: "Personalized learning is exactly what it sounds like. It means connecting lessons to students' communities and cultures. It is about cultivating agency by listening to students when they say what they need."[28] How does personalized learning connect lessons to students' communities and cultures? "Integrating social-emotional development into academic lessons improves student behavior which leads to greater content knowledge and motivation to learn."[29] In other words, social and emotional learning and other resilience programs promise learned self-regulation for students to consume knowledge and adapt to existing realities. The progressive rhetoric suggests something other than a repackaged and technologized form of transmissional pedagogy or banking education in which knowledge is seen as a commodity to be delivered by the technology and consumed by the student. "We define learner success by strong academic outcomes, growth mindset, 21st century skills (including relationship, problem-solving, self-management, and leadership skills), and wider, denser webs of support, as well as social capital."[30]

Leap claims to be promoting personalization while being utterly inattentive to student subjectivity and cultural differences. That's because it is actually about quantification of affect and behavior to commercialize them as data, the repackaging of the standards and accountability movement's transmission model of pedagogy under the guise of technological innovation and individual choice. This is part of an agenda to quantify and commercialize student behavior and affect deep privatization. The shift from venture philanthropy to digital privatization represents a shift in direction for the educational privatization movement. It also represents a reworking of the uses of education for the social and cultural reproduction of capital. It signifies the building of new techno-tracking and commercial longitudinal surveillance which is part of the new directions of the political economy of schooling and the broader expansion of surveillance capitalism.[31]

Like a number of other companies promoting digital privatization of education through resilience, Leap Innovations has come to appropriate a number of key terms that have historically been developed by critical education scholars. Critical education scholars have used these terms to explain how education is implicated in reproducing a racialized class hierarchy, that is, how it recreates society and recreates social inequality. In critical education traditions, knowledge, curriculum, and culture are political in that they represent the particular views, ideologies, and interests of particular groups and are subject to struggle and contestation by these groups who have incommensurate symbolic and material interests and social positions. Recently, corporations and foundations that produce knowledge in support of their educational profit-seeking work have been appropriating critical educational language. For example, the Lego Foundation which produces advocacy literature to justify Lego's business of play-based learning misappropriates the language of agency and cultural relevance.

Leap Innovation claims its programs are "personalized." What this means is that "by definition, personalized learning allows students to move at their own pace through material."[32] According to the director of Research of Leap, Amy Nowell,

> if students aim to learn a particular unit within a specified period of time and the product provides feedback that "you have only completed one activity" in that time frame, what, she asked, does that mean to a student trying to complete and comprehend the full unit?

The point not to be missed here is that this personalized learning platform has a finite number of standardized lessons. Students can move faster or slower through these lessons, but the lessons do not change to engage in dialogue and debate with students or to make learning socially engaged by relating claims to truth to broader relations of authority. The lessons are filled with standardized tests purporting to be objective, neutral, and disinterested measures of learning of curriculum that is also purported to be objective, neutral, and disinterested. What "personalized" does not mean is that the lessons or curriculum relates to the students' culture, knowledge, prior experience, or other aspects of their subjectivity such as their class, race, or gender positions. What "personalized" also does not mean in Leap Innovations' curriculum is that learning is related to understanding claims to truth in relation to the particular interests of the claimant or relating the curriculum to the broader interests, values, and ideologies of the ones making the curriculum and the built-in tests. That is, "personalization" as taken up by Leap fails to interrogate how actual persons make knowledge and how the decisions about what to include or exclude from lessons relate to perspectives and interests that go beyond individuals, representing, rather, the perspectives and interests of ruling groups. This "personalization" also fails to show how knowledge—misrepresented as neutral, objective, and universal—is, in fact, political, subjectively grounded, and struggled over by different classes and cultural groups.

Leap claims its personalized learning platform promotes "agency." Personalized learning "is about cultivating agency by listening to students when they say what they need."[33]

Leap lays out its three "Grounding Principles" on its website Leapinnovations.org:

- Every Learner Can Succeed with Support That's Customized to the Child's Interests and Needs
- Every Learner Brings Strengths and Talents to the Classroom
- Learner Agency Is Essential
- Our world of work increasingly requires more leadership, agility and self-direction. At an early age, we must inspire our students to assume responsibility of their own learning, and help co-design it.

Such assumption of responsibility for learning and "co-designing" learning does not mean what it means for critical education traditions. Those traditions relate learning to student experience and help students comprehend how experience is socially formed. The critical understanding of the self and society becomes the basis for political agency to aspire to challenge and transform oppression and the social forces and institutions that produce it. Leap Innovations empties the critical concept of agency of any meaning as it actually refers to students using an automated computer program to learn a standardized curriculum that is incapable of addressing public problems that students experience, social forces and oppression. Agency does not mean the capacity to comprehend and act on oppressive forces. It means here speeding up or slowing down canned curriculum programs. This is a conception of agency that is at best about a false promise of economic agency within consumer capitalism, agency as worker or consumer, not a political conception of agency that is about social comprehension for collective action to intervene in public problems.

What Is Personalized Learning?

At Leap, our definition of personalized learning lies within the construct of the LEAP Learning Framework's four core components: Personalized learning is FOCUSED on, LED with and DEMONSTRATED by the learner, and is CONNECTED TO career-relevant, real world skills and opportunities.[34]

Despite the overblown rhetoric of agency, the teaching of automated canned curriculum is very much in line with the long corporate education project of school to work. This is an instrumental and vocational conception of learning in which the student efficiently consumed knowledge prescribed by the ones who know rather than co-creating knowledge through dialogic exchange.

Leap also empties out the critical education concept of "praxis." Praxis in critical education is about the process of reflective action. Teachers help students theorize the experience of oppression through the curriculum, and this reconceptualization of experience forms the basis for a different understanding and action on the forces that produce the experience of oppression. Leap Innovations claims its programs employ "praxis."

> We developed the Framework with the same four-phase "Praxis" Design Methodology that we use each time to re-evaluate or add to it. "Praxis" refers to the practical application of a theory, which for LEAP means we apply learning science and research to the contexts of educators. The structured approach to refining our work ensures that all of our ideas continue to be firmly rooted in real-world evidence, and powered by the diversity of perspective we've seen deliver success.[35]

Leap's appropriation of "praxis" transformed the concept from one that is about education as the process of social understanding toward the end of social intervention and transformation to being about teaching methods for instilling knowledge. Whereas the critical education traditions see the process of theorizing particular social contexts and experiences as the basis for a new understanding and collective social action, Leap sees "praxis" as a narrow methodological approach that aims for teachers to refine their teaching methods to "deliver" a body of knowledge to students. Whereas "praxis" in the critical education tradition involves the co-creation of knowledge through dialogic exchange between teachers and students, Leap's conception rebrands a technological version of banking education in which knowledge is not co-created but imparted and imposed. Leap's rhetoric about "learning science" and "research" demonstrates their embrace of the guise of disinterested objectivity and their concomitant denial of the politics of knowledge and the politics of pedagogy recognized by the critical education tradition.

The critical tradition makes the politics of knowledge and curriculum central to the process of teaching and learning in that they represent the particular perspectives and interests of classes and cultural groups. Leap empties the language of "praxis" of any sense of the relationships between knowledge and power. The critical tradition helps students analyze and interpret how knowledge-making practices secure forms of social authority, suggest particular kinds of social relations, and proffer particular identifications and subject positions.[36]

This chapter has illustrated that some of the key players of venture philanthropy who promoted school privatization and neoliberal district restructuring have expanded their privatization initiatives into digital educational privatization. Resilience concepts and product content have been central to the new digital directions of the venture philanthropists. As well, this chapter illustrated how part of the uses of resilience discourse that includes the misappropriation of critical and progressive education language has become commonplace in selling digital education contracts. Whereas this chapter examined how resilience is deeply implicated in the new terrain of educational privatization at the scale of the school and the curriculum, the next chapter focuses on the extent to which the concept of trauma undergirds resilience education projects.

5

Trauma-Informed Pedagogy

In the past decade, trauma-informed pedagogy has become nearly omnipresent in schools and in the field of education. Trauma-informed pedagogy trainings and advocacy material on the web far outnumber scholarship on it. However, there is a growing body of scholarly literature about it. Most of the scholarship relies on the same set of conceptual assumptions and purports to be grounded in a couple of empirical studies. Trauma-informed pedagogy is one of many resilience pedagogy programs that *appear* to buck the legacy of the standards and accountability movement. Resilience theories like trauma-informed pedagogy seemingly attend to subjective concerns ignored and denied by the objectivism of the standards and accountability movement. For example, trauma-informed pedagogy like social and emotional learning, personalized learning, meditation programs, and mindfulness seems to put the self at the center of teaching and learning. However, upon closer examination trauma-informed pedagogy has the same ultimate aims as the standards and accountability movement—improving transmission models of pedagogy, that is, the delivery of allegedly disinterested objective knowledge, by unblocking the self. Trauma-informed pedagogy shares the same animating assumptions with other resilience programs and projects such as the teaching of grit—a program that employs behaviorist techniques to encourage learned self-control in the face of educational drudgery.

Trauma-informed pedagogy strings together a series of assumptions and assertions to make the case for lessons in learned self-control toward the end of the consumption of knowledge. This learned self-control is supposed to facilitate getting students to learn knowledge that is prescribed by standards but is not necessarily meaningful or relevant. In other words, trauma-informed pedagogy aims for the efficient transmission of knowledge by purporting to overcome psychological and physiological blockages to students' submission to the authority of the teacher and acceptance of the curriculum. Trauma-informed pedagogy does not see learning as dialogical and knowledge as co-created through dialogue by teachers and students as do other educational traditions such as constructivism, democratic education, and critical pedagogy. Instead, trauma-informed pedagogy treats knowledge as a thing or commodity to be consumed and defines learning as healthy adaptation to the imposition of knowledge and defines unhealthy dispositions as those that do not adapt to the authority of the teacher and prescribed knowledge. While transmission models of pedagogy are hardly new, what makes trauma-informed pedagogy unique is the bringing together of a biological definition of trauma as a blockage to transmission and the advocacy of techniques of learned self-control to overcome the physiology of trauma. Moreover, many of the digital resilience products and programs that are justified on the basis of trauma-informed pedagogy are structured for constant testing and teaching to the test. Such products represent a growing and highly lucrative for-profit industry in resilience.

The common narrative of trauma-informed pedagogy expressed in the scholarship goes like this:

1) Trauma is the result of adverse childhood experiences. The literature on trauma-informed pedagogy makes recourse to one 1997 study of Adverse Childhood Experiences (the ACEs study) which found "youth who had experienced higher 'doses' of ACEs (categorized as abuse, household challenges, or neglect) before they were 18 went on to face greater rates of depression, drug use, physiological disease (including cancer and cardiovascular disease), risk for intimate partner violence, financial instability, and poor academic achievement as adults."[1]

2) Toxic Stress. This childhood trauma from adverse childhood experiences results in "toxic stress" which is physiological and

explains that psychological distress becomes physical as a result of excess release of cortisol and adrenaline in the bodies of students.[2]

3) Toxic Stress Threatens Learning. Students with toxic stress are alleged to have trouble learning because they lack adequate self-regulation, that is, self-control. And in the positive psychology spin on trauma-informed pedagogy, toxic stress also threatens social relationships called "attachments."

4) Schools need mental health resources but in their place trauma-informed pedagogy can be infused into the curriculum.

5) Resilience Products to the Rescue. Resilience products and programs such as Grit, Growth Mindset, and Digital Mindfulness, and Meditation Programs such as Buddhify, Calm, GoNoodle, Headspace, Insight Timer[3] promise to counter toxic stress, give students self-control and hence allow them to learn prescribed curriculum. That is, resilience programs such as this purport to create the physiological and mental conditions for adaptation to the prescribed curriculum and pedagogy and the undoing of what the literature calls "non-adaptive coping strategies."

Upon examination each piece of the five-part narrative is dubious and falls apart.

1) Adverse Childhood Experiences. While experiences of "abuse, household challenges, or neglect" represent violent conditions to which no child should be subjected, the framing of the problems in this way abstracts the experience of adversity from the broader social forces and structures that produce it. Consequently, individual experiences of trauma appear as causes of future life and educational outcomes rather than recognizing that those outcomes correlate with broader patterns of social organization rather than familial or individual behavior. For example, a racialized class hierarchy produces poverty, inequality, and symbolic violence that increases both the likelihood of "abuse, household challenges, or neglect" and the likelihood of the effects these traumatic conditions purport to cause: "depression, drug use, physiological

disease (including cancer and cardiovascular disease), risk for intimate partner violence, financial instability, and poor academic achievement as adults."[4] There are important consequences of framing the origins of trauma through individual experience and behavior as opposed to the structural forces that inform experience and behavior. It results in the solution to the problem being sought in individualized ways that are incapable of addressing the causes of the violence. The intervention is not to stop the poverty, inequality, and symbolic violence through public action, policy, and educative projects. Rather, the solution is sought through interventions made to the victims of violence rather than the violent context. As well, this individualized conception of the meaning of trauma forecloses the possibility of forms of treatment that help traumatized individuals reconceptualize the meaning of traumatic experiences and hence rework the experience itself by learning the broader social, political, and historical causes of traumatic situations (later in this chapter I discuss Gabor Maté and critical pedagogy as examples).

The Adverse Childhood Experiences study is also deeply problematic in how it frames trauma. Tom Brunzell, Helen Stokes, and Lea Waters, prolific authors on trauma-informed pedagogy, offer a standard definition of trauma:

> Trauma can be defined as an overwhelming experience that undermines one's belief that the world is good or safe and can dramatically and negatively affect a student's educational trajectory. (Downey, 2007)[5]

This definition of trauma depends upon a fantasy of childhood innocence and ignorance. Most rational adults willing to face the abundant evidence around us do not believe that the world is either inherently good or that it is safe. We are bombarded daily by news and information about the environmental and climate disasters of global warming and the short time horizon to mitigate imminent global catastrophe, the worsening dangers of nuclear proliferation, the global receding of democracy as political formation and ideal, the worsening of global poverty and inequality and the vast amassing of wealth at the top of the economy, the realities of the Covid-19 pandemic, the increasing visibility of scapegoating and violent racist attacks by police and white supremacists, and others. Indeed, the lack of adequate educational means, the critical tools for understanding and acting to stop the causes of these catastrophes, leaves people in a state of disorientation, confusion, and political illiteracy that renders them vulnerable to easy answers and emotionally potent simplifications of conspiracy theories. Who, we must ask, is able to be kept hermetically sealed in a bubble and not be exposed either to the effects of these realities or knowledge of these realities?

The reality is that the world is not inherently good or safe but learning can be a means of striving to make it so. That is, learning can be comprehended as a means of political and social agency to act on the very problems that make the world unsafe. The definition of trauma in trauma-informed pedagogy presumes that there is no relationship between education and comprehension of the broader social forces, structures, and antagonisms which produce the conditions one experiences as traumatic. Trauma is a subjectively experienced effect of broader social forces and public problems. TIP translates trauma into a strictly private, often familial, psychological rather than social reality.

These points are in no way a dismissal of the experience of trauma. The very real experience of trauma needs to be comprehended in relation to the social totality that produces the conditions for violence, and that makes experience meaningful as trauma. The intervention in such a social rather than individual framing can become the means of responding by seeking to act on and change the social conditions that produce trauma rather than only seeking to salve the wounds of the self. Many children, particularly from oppressed groups, grow up around adults who educate them about their own histories of oppression, the history of the oppression of others, and various means people have used over the course of history to resist, oppose, or overturn such oppression. Children benefit from understanding that social reality is more complicated than the idea that one ought to always trust authority.

2) Toxic Stress. Trauma-informed pedagogy, by explaining trauma as biological, naturalizes trauma to justify control. Excess cortisol and adrenaline production become causes of a condition posed as a blockage to learning. Trauma-informed pedagogy is at odds with critical pedagogy and its emphasis on theorizing experience to understand how it is socially produced and that such theorization can be the basis for a new understanding and agency. In critical pedagogy, experience, including the experience of trauma, can become an object of critical analysis taken up in relation to the broader social realities that produce it. In trauma-informed pedagogy, the biological explanation becomes the justification not for dialogue-based interventions oriented around co-creating knowledge and understanding the relationship between the self and the society but rather the justification for body control and repressive pedagogies that are framed as "adaptive strategies."[6] Such control is in the service to anti-intellectual and anti-critical transmission models of pedagogy.

3) Toxic Stress Threatens Learning. Students with toxic stress are alleged to have trouble learning because they lack adequate self-regulation, that is, self-control. Jennifer Bashant's *Building a Trauma-Informed Compassionate Classroom* provides a concise illustration of how trauma-informed pedagogy purports to work to get a student to control himself. As Bashant instructs the teacher in her book, "Your number one priority when a student is exhibiting challenging behavior is to help them become regulated."[7] A teacher worksheet titled "Current Self-Regulation Strategies" instructs the teacher to "assess the type of self-regulation strategies that the student is currently using," in order to identify "non-adaptive strategies" and teach the student "adaptive strategies" in their place. The worksheet lists a number of "nonadaptive strategies," including "running out of the classroom," "refusal or defiance," "silliness," "arguing and/or cursing," "physical aggression," "daydreaming," "avoidance and/or shutting down." The teacher is supposed to examine these behaviors, determine the "purpose that each strategy serves for the student," and then work with the student to "select an adaptive strategy to replace each nonadaptive strategy."

The worksheet offers the following as "adaptive strategies": "Taking deep breaths," "Listening to calming music," Taking a walk," "Talking with a trusted adult," "Asking for help," "Exercise and/or heavy work," "Swinging/Rocking."

Part of what is remarkable and disturbing in a program such as this is that it provides no sense for how the teacher is to interpret the student's behavior. Is the student's "refusal" or "defiance" to do the work that the teacher imposes a matter of the student's past trauma or a matter of the work being meaningless and unrelated to anything that the student might find meaningful or relevant or valuable? Is the student's "avoidance/shutting down" about some past trauma or a matter of the classroom being experienced as "dead time" because the curriculum appears decontextualized and meaningless? Is "daydreaming" or "silliness" a symptom of a past trauma or an outlet for the student's creativity which the curriculum and pedagogical approach does not allow? Is "aggression" or "running out of the classroom" a symptom of trauma or an act of opposition and resistance to an educational context that is experienced as oppressive, an imposition, or even potentially as a form of state-imposed violence against working-class and poor students and non-white students? In *Theory and Resistance in Education*, Henry Giroux analyzed how this kind of resistance may be political and needs to be comprehended in relation to broader class and cultural group antagonisms and dynamics. For Giroux there is a pedagogical opportunity in working with students to comprehend their resistance; this is an opportunity to develop critical consciousness by analyzing how the experience is socially produced.

Bashant's program offers nothing to answer any of these crucial questions but rather assumes that in every case the student's behavior is a symptom of a past trauma. Yet, if it is a function of a past trauma, the program provides no way for the teacher to engage with the student about the traumatic experience or the immediate or broader social causes of it. On its own terms, the program provides no means for the teacher to comprehend the student behavior or relate the interpreted behavior to the proposed adaptive strategies. However, the "adaptive strategies" such as deep breathing or listening to soothing music have no relationship to interpreting or acting on the situation at hand. Lastly, it is completely unclear how these advocated practices relate to student learning other than as allegedly creating conditions to make students into passive receptacles for prescribed knowledge. Whereas critical pedagogy relates learning to both student experience and broader social realities such that knowledge becomes an instrument of self and social empowerment, trauma-informed pedagogy does neither.

4) TIP serves in place of absent mental health resources. As the aforementioned illustrates, what is going by the moniker trauma-informed pedagogy is hardly coherent as educational practice let alone a replacement for mental health resources that have been eroded since the early 1980s and decades of the neoliberal gutting of the caregiving state institutions such as public mental hospitals. Yet, mental health needs have expanded as caregiving and social support roles of the state have been scaled back even more and repression and inequality have worsened violent conditions and atomization for youth. Schools, administrators, and teachers have been positioned as behavioral health practitioners despite these workers not being specialists and despite this dividing these educators' time.[8]

5) The solution to trauma is sought in apps and digital products as well as other contracted programs that purport to make resilient students who will be compliant. The aforementioned example from Bashant's book is but one illustration. She encourages her readers to purchase products both digital and analogue. These products target students, parents, teachers, and district contracts. They sell "mindfulness" and calm to counter "toxic stress": Mindful Arts Activity Cards, Rain Sticks, Tibetan Singing Bowls, apps: Buddhify, Calm, GoNoodle, Headspace, Insight Timer.[9] It is noteworthy that many of these mindfulness, meditation, social and emotional learning, and calm products trade in quasi-spirituality. They appropriate spiritual symbols to extract practices that are intended to modify and control student bodies. The practices are decontextualized from their origins. For example, meditation is decontextualized, removed from the larger

Buddhist spiritual tradition (to name one of many) that emphasizes the abdication of desire, non-attachment to material things on the path to enlightenment and freedom. Meditation and mindfulness techniques in the resilience market abstracts these practices and, in accordance with the broader industry in new age products (trading in happiness, positivity, and self-help[10]), transforms them into personal effectiveness techniques and techniques of control. The point of these techniques is to target the body to make the student "ready to learn" which means ready to be a willing receptacle for deposited knowledge.

These techniques are recontextualized as the proper inheritor of the standards and accountability movement intended to make students into subjects of greater capacity. Seemingly attentive to the student's subjectivity by emphasizing the student's behavior and affect, trauma-informed pedagogy in fact disregards students' experiences, cultures, and social positions. It delinks knowledge and learning from the most significant aspects of subjectivity and retains the standards and accountability treatment of knowledge as a static thing that is made by others elsewhere—the ones who know. Leaning in this discourse is not a means of social comprehension, and knowledge is not a means of social power. Trauma-informed pedagogy fails to provide a means for students to investigate their own real traumas and the broader social causes that produce the conditions for those traumas because it makes trauma into physical symptoms and treats trauma through techniques to soothe or control the body.

Trauma-informed pedagogy as an instrument of control for transmission models of pedagogy recasts what historically was understood economically and politically as the imperatives of social and cultural reproduction of capital. As critical sociologists of education explain, schooling in the industrial economy (for most of the twentieth century) served in part to teach what they called the "hidden curriculum" of capitalism.[11] This hidden curriculum taught skills and know-how for students to take prescribed places in the labor force but wrapped in ideologies that taught social relationships conducive to those prescribed labor roles. These lessons were different based on the different class position of the students. For example, working-class and poor students learned largely basic skills and dispositions for obedience to authority. Learning to obey the teacher set the stage for learning to obey the boss later. Professional class students largely learned academic skills and knowledge to prepare them to manage industry for the ruling class. These students learned the dispositions of curiosity, dialogue, debate, dissent for them to take their place in leadership roles in the public and private sector.

As Henry Giroux has pointed out, by the 1990s the "hidden curriculum" was no longer hidden. By the advent of neoliberalism in the 1980s, the imperatives of schooling for capitalism were on the surface. Working-class students still learned basic skills and obedience to authority in the form of learned self-control but in ideological forms that overtly celebrated corporate culture and framed students as primarily future workers. The standardization, homogenization, and enforcement of curriculum through testing became ubiquitous as did dressing students in uniforms that made them look like big box retail workers. Control of working-class students' bodies also took an increasingly carceral and militarized form with the expansion of metal detectors, police presence, and surveillance. As well, control included drugging working-class kids into obedience to authority with stimulant drugs justified on the grounds of increasing student test scores. Meanwhile professional class students increasingly learned forms of self-control that made them "students of capacity" to manage their own bodies with emotional and attentional regulation drugs such as Xanax and Ritalin. In the neoliberal era, the reproductive role of schooling for capitalism changed somewhat, focusing less on making workers whose labor exploitation could form the basis for profit and more on making students into commodities for whom contracting arrangements would create profit or made disposable, outside of the needs of the larger economic context. Charters, vouchers, and contracting schemes became a much more direct way for capitalists to extract profit from public schooling. Digital privatization, facilitated by resilience discourse, takes this further.

Trauma-informed pedagogy and other resilience pedagogies are part of a contemporary reworking of the imperatives of social and cultural reproduction in education. Resilience pedagogies serve to reproduce the conditions for capital accumulation in several ways. They continue the long-standing narrative that educational reform, rather than economic redistribution, is responsible for ameliorating poverty and economic inequality. They emphasize learned self-control and particular forms of self-discipline toward the end of learning skills and know-how for work. They also teach ideologies of self-blame and self-cure for adverse social conditions. They help shift the onus for humane social conditions away from those most able to fund them and onto those who are the victims of policies and laws that enshrine inequality. Ideologically, they also crucially emphasize adaptation to worsening social and economic and environmental conditions rather than political engagement or contestation to change the institutions and structures that would foster greater human security and egalitarian and democratic economic relationships. Trauma-informed pedagogy and other resilience pedagogies also create the conditions for new forms of educational privatization and school commercialism by justifying the expansion of digital software and curriculum that not only creates contracting profits for investors but transforms student behavior into lucrative data and makes students into data production engines. The data produced by these apps is a commodity that is widely traded and circulated as it has the potential to be run through big data algorithms with predictive power, forming consumer profiling identities. As Jathan Sadowski points out, data has commercial value for its unforeseen future potential uses.[12]

"How Did We All Become Traumatized?"

Trauma has become a near-universal experience and social category. Fiction author and social critic Will Self asks, "How everything became trauma."[13] Self answers the question by tracing the history of trauma's modern origins in Freud, its definition through war and technology.[14] Today's conceptions of trauma are radically different from the concept's origins in Freud. For Freud, a traumatic experience, such as witnessing one's parents having sex, was repressed. The repression of traumatic experience would potentially result in neurotic symptoms. Freud developed the talking cure for the traumatized person to unburden themself of the repressed trauma by recounting it or engaging in a variety of techniques that would bring the repressed memory of trauma to the surface of the conscious mind.

Trauma took a number of turns through history manifesting in various illnesses ranging from nineteenth-century female-gendered hysteria to twentieth-century male-gendered post-traumatic stress disorder. In education, historically trauma has played a significant role in the development of ideas of adolescence and middle school that persist today (e.g., adolescence as a distinct period of development, "storm and stress"). In the late nineteenth and early twentieth centuries, G. Stanley Hall developed a widely embraced concept known as "recapitulation theory."[15] Recapitulation theory held that the development of the human being follows or recapitulates the history of the human species. Hall embraced the European developmental idea of the great chain of being with civilization developing from nature to animality to primitive humanity to civilized humanity. Hall's thoroughly racist, classist, and sexist model presumed that civilization was being led by white men and that the future depended upon the successful development of white professional- and ruling-class boys who could lead humanity. However, Hall worried about the stresses of modern industrial civilization (storm and stress) taxing the nervous energies of these white boys. To be strengthened for the task ahead, white boys would need to go back down the chain of civilization temporarily to draw on the power of the primitive to get toughened up. The Boy Scouts and the YMCA were some of the organizations that would provide the conduit back to primitive nature for white boys to draw on the power of the repressed.

Since Hall, middle-level education has largely retained the narrative of "storm and stress" that needs to be overcome for healthy development.

Hall's perspective shared with the Freudian legacy a view of trauma in which the original traumatic event was repressed to the conscious mind. Freud proposed techniques such as transference which would allow the "patient" to "work through" the trauma and translate it into a narrative that would possibly take a different turn. This supposedly would allow the patient to come to terms with and process the trauma and address the symptoms.

In these views, the society itself followed the same path as the traumatized individual (recapitulation). For Freud, as he explains in *Civilization and Its Discontents*, repression of instinctual drives for violence and sex is necessary and "the price of civilization." In other words, a certain level of repression is necessary for civilization to keep in check the instincts. But too much repression results in neurosis and dysfunction. Hall's recapitulation theory calls on youth to recover repressed and forgotten stages of the primitive brutal human past by going into nature and then bringing this repressed and forgotten primitive power forward and incorporating it into contemporary life, the heights of civilized competition. We still see this logic in the naming of warfighting weapons (Apache helicopters, Tomahawk Missiles) and sports teams for indigenous people and animals.

Contemporary narratives about trauma have largely abandoned the assumption that the original cause of trauma was necessarily repressed. The mystery at the center of the trauma that needed to be recovered through psychoanalysis, hypnosis, or taking to the woods and reenacting "primitive" rituals has now been replaced with the project of scientific recovery of the foundation of trauma. The grounding of trauma as a biological effect of stress measured in cortisol and adrenaline excess appears to offer a definitive, quantifiable, and scientific explanation to trauma. Yet, the scientific explanation offers nothing to explain how and why a given experience becomes traumatic to a particular person or how acts of interpretation can transform a person's understanding of the meaning of the trauma they experience, for example, by ideologically, socially, and politically situating it.

What is notably different about early twentieth-century discourses of trauma threatening human and social development from the discourse of trauma-informed pedagogy is their conceptions of human agency. For G. Stanley Hall the aim of toughening up little white boys by going back to nature so that they did not succumb to the perils of modern nerve-wracking industrial life was to make strong agents capable of leading humanity forward. While this vision was defined through white supremacy, eurocentrism, misogyny, and primitivism, it nonetheless construed trauma as a *social* illness (the nerve-wracking stresses of modern industrial society) and the child (not all children, only white boys) as needing to be able to shape and control and direct the social world of the future for progress. In the resilience discourse of trauma-informed pedagogy, trauma is socially originating too but the only hope of trauma-informed pedagogy is for the individual to adapt to bad social conditions. In this view, poverty, violence, and inequality cannot be addressed except as subjectively lived corporeal symptoms in the traumatized person.

One notable exception is contemporary advocate for trauma-informed practice, psychiatrist and social critic Gabor Maté, who explains the need for trauma to be comprehended within the social totality.[16] In this view, in a culture that is atomizing, alienating, violent, and characterized by radical inequality, trauma can be understood as the psychic wound that results from catastrophic events and conditions. Responding to the vast increases in youth mental illness and suicide, particularly during the Covid-19 pandemic, Maté says,

> Now, we can make two assumptions. Either there's some accidental, totally unexplainable rise in childhood pathology that has no specific reason whatsoever for its instigation, or we can recognize that we live in a toxic culture that, by its very nature, affects children development in such unhealthy ways that children are increasingly mentally unbalanced and desperate to the extent that they're cutting themselves and even trying to kill themselves. So, we have to look for those conditions, not in the individual mind or brain or personality of the child or youth; we have to look at them in the social conditions that drive children in those directions. And unfortunately, in the public conversation around it, it's all about the pathology and how to treat it,

and it's not about the social or cultural causes that are driving children in those desperate directions.[17]

Maté's willingness to socially situate trauma is vastly preferable to the plethora of trauma programs that treat trauma as individual subjective pathology. Maté's view suggests addressing trauma both by the process of understanding the origins of trauma in the self and by comprehending the social conditions that inform and give rise to traumatic events. Maté's view provides an indispensable dimension to conceptualizing a trauma-informed pedagogy that would take seriously the social formation of the self.

However, there are limitations to Maté's perspective. One problem is that he inflates trauma so that it becomes a universal explanation for social ills, going so far as to explain capitalism as an effect of trauma. While racial capitalism certainly produces a tremendous amount of trauma, and the subjective effects of capitalist and racist violence surely become further commodified, to project causality from subjective trauma to the formation of social structure is dubious. Rather, subjectivity and social structure dialectically produce each other. Another problem for Maté is the tenuous claim that physical illness such as cancer is a consequence of trauma. While there is scientific evidence to support the claim that emotional states have real physiological effects, to claim as he does that a woman with stage four uterine cancer who was a rape victim suffered from "rape cancer" and was healed through trauma therapy is to potentially reduce all cancer and other illness to manifestations of trauma and to overly emphasize the power of emotional states in physical health. Another of the major problems with Maté's account of trauma is that in the tradition of ego psychology he frames the self as ideally authentic and cohesive and trauma as threatening this true self. This stands in contrast not only to psychoanalytic accounts but also to post-structural views of selfhood that recognize that the self is never self-same and that identity is not fixed but is formed by the process of identification—which happens through learning. Because the self is always pedagogically shaped through the process of identification, cultural representations, and shifting discourses form the ideological inventory from which the self is composed.[18] Two mid-twentieth-century theorists of identity, Erich Fromm and Erik Erikson, in different ways recognized that identity is non-identical because of human development and the ongoing processes of individuation. Both comprehended that the individual repeatedly goes through periods of crisis in which they individuate from figures of authority. Fromm in particular saw rationality itself having its formation in early expressions of the refusal of parental authority. The child's "no" is a moment of separation from parents, individuation, and the beginning of thinking for oneself. In these theories while healthy development results from the development of autonomy of the self, the self is never fixed or self-same in its autonomy. As well, these theories see trauma not as an exceptional event but as integral to the development of the self as the self develops healthy individuation in relating to others: neither the masochistic abdication of the self to another nor the sadistic pursuit of controlling others as objects.[19] Paulo Freire, in drawing on Fromm, elaborates the concept of adhesion in which the self sees through the eyes of the oppressor. The ongoing problem-posing practice of critical pedagogy aims for critical consciousness formation in part by making an object of the self in the world, estranging that objectified self, critically analyzing experience, and establishing a different sense of self and world. Such critical practice expands agency—a sense of the capacity to understand and act on the world. Understanding in this context involves reinterpreting one's experience by socially situating it—including reinterpreting traumatic experience. This perspective on trauma is contrary to those that existentialize trauma as permanent and inevitable features of an identity mistakenly conceived as fixed.

Critical theories of self also take up trauma and selfhood differently than both trauma-informed pedagogy and ego psychology with their overly unified conceptions of the individual. In such theories, social reality and consciousness are ideologically structured such that consciousness is mediated through ideology. There is no authentic self or outside to ideology/discourse. One sees this perspective of ideological subjectivity formation in a number of social and educational theories in the critical education legacy. These theories see ideological subjectivity formation in relation to class and political economy. Examples include Antonio Gramsci, Louis Althusser, Stuart Hall, Raymond Williams, Ernesto Laclau, Chantal Mouffe, Henry Giroux, and Stanley Aronowitz, to name a few. Critical psychoanalytic feminist educational theorists such as Sharon Todd and Deborah Britzman also recognize a self constituted by difference. The self and the society are symbolic and characterized by a gap or lack at their core. In contrast to the assumption of a cohesive authentic self, such a gap or lack at the core of the self makes possible the development of new forms of consciousness through learning and identification. As well, such a view recognizes the extent to which the meaning of the body cannot be grounded or guaranteed by the body's biology or materiality. The meaning of the body is symbolic and ideology or discourse allows for the materiality of the body to be made part of broader meanings and narratives about people. Identity positions such as race, gender, sexuality, and so on are fictions, social constructions, but fictions with real material effects. Critical pedagogies denaturalize oppressive ideologies and identifications and suggest better ideologies and identifications. Critical pedagogies help to reveal how trauma is produced as not just material effects but as consequences of meaning-making activity situated in broader social and political formations and dependent upon acts of interpretation and judgment. While Maté sees the treatment of trauma in largely the same way as a kind of self and social "disillusionment," the assumption of trauma as a wound or lack that can be healed to restore the wholeness of self, offers a limited perspective. The self and society are ideological, in formation, fragmented, constituted by difference and non-identity, not guaranteed, and consequently open to being pedagogically remade.

From Resilience to the Culture
of Democracy

Globally, democracy is in dire peril. Around the world numerous formerly democratic nations have fallen prey to authoritarianism while oftentimes democratically elected leaders aspire to erode democratic electoral processes, civil liberties, participation, and norms. Fascist political parties are on the rise, and numerous global indexes of democracy and freedom indicate a steady decline in democracy in the past decade as measured, for example, by electoral process, functioning of government, civil liberties, political participation, and democratic culture.[1] The last of these, democratic culture, depends upon educative institutions to be cultivated and fostered. Only 6 percent of the world's population is now living in one of the twenty-one nations designated as a full democracy.[2] Since 2016 the United States has been listed as a flawed democracy, and countless scholars and analysts are sounding the alarm that the United States is moving toward authoritarianism. Numerous civil liberties including speech, right to protest, academic freedom at all levels, and voting have been significantly reduced, while mechanisms to ensure free and fair elections have been undermined by the political right. These include the equation of money with political speech that allows corporations and the superrich to purchase election outcomes as decided by the US Supreme Court's *Citizens United* decision. Democratic norms have been drastically eroded, including acceptance of election outcomes, respect for rule of law, and belief in the legitimacy of the government and public institutions. Sheldon Wolin described the current situation as "inverted totalitarianism," while Henry Giroux explained the decline of democracy as owing to the expansion of "neoliberal fascism."[3]

The prior chapters have illustrated that resilience discourse has a number of harms. Some of these are exemplary of a culture where a long tradition of democratic governance is becoming unstable. They include the replacement of political agency with adaptation to the world as it is, a shifting of the onus for addressing inequality, poverty, exclusion, and social violence onto the individual, the promotion of selfhood that cannot account for the ways the self is socially formed, and a disregard for the relationship between the self and social forces and struggles. In addition, in education, resilience has become a lubricant to get repressive and for-profit technologies into classrooms and to create the conditions for educational markets in contracting and data extraction with questionable educational benefit. Such educational profiteering drains public resources out of the educational process. This concluding chapter contends that there is an additional harm: the displacement of intellectual traditions and practices crucial for a democratic society. That is, resilience discourse expands as scholarship, knowledge, educational values, and cultural politics that are essential to democratic modes of education recede. Resilience discourse such as social emotional learning and personalized learning/adaptive learning technology is involved in the expansion of standardized testing as curriculum. The expansion of resilience programs in the curriculum comes at the expense of the displacement of literature, history, and other interpretive humanities and social science traditions as well as critical educational practices in K–12 schools. Resilience programs sell these curriculum and pedagogy trends under a promise of moving away from excessive testing, the standards and accountability movement, and attention to the personal. They appear to be contrary to the hierarchical, authoritarian, and anti-dialogic standards and accountability movement. The opposite is the case. The last section of the chapter expands the discussion about the decontextualization of the subject and displacement of intellectual traditions by resilience pedagogies to the recent spectacle of critical race theory.

Democratic societies depend upon the educated citizenry. Education provides the means for citizens to develop knowledge and democratic dispositions for collective self-governance. Both what knowledge students should learn and what constitutes a democratic disposition are profoundly political and hotly disputed across the political spectrum. A democratic approach to culture does not deposit a canon of the right knowledge but rather provides students with the means to learn through interpretation and dialogue with others and reading texts of various traditions. Democracy demands dispositions of dialogue, debate, dissent, and curiosity.

Education plays a crucial role in providing not just facts but the intellectual tools to interpret claims to truth in relation to their conditions of production. That is, in a democracy students need to not merely accumulate knowledge but develop the capacities to comprehend how knowledge relates to power, how knowledge is made through meaning-making exchange, what values, assumptions, and ideologies undergird claims to truth, and they need to develop the capacity to analyze how material and symbolic interests and social tendencies animate claims to truth. Curriculum is inherently political in that particular people with particular ideological and social positions, values, and interests make curriculum. Certain educational techniques shut down the capacity of students to see and engage the politics of curriculum. For example, standardized testing purports to test knowledge that is neutral, disinterested, and of universal value while obscuring the selection and framing of questions and answers. What has disappeared in the standardized testing process are the interests, ideologies, and values of the test makers as well as the ways that the interests, ideologies, and values of the test takers inform their interpretation of the tests. The process of knowledge-making appears as a seamless transmission, a depositing of neutral knowledge from the ones who know to the ones who do not know rather than knowledge-making through dialogic exchange in which some parties have more power to make meanings than others. Within this testing ritual students cannot question or challenge or debate the knowledge makers who composed the test. They are denied the opportunity to question why this knowledge matters as opposed to other knowledge.

Democratic approaches to knowledge and education are particularly under siege in the United States as right-wing populists aggressively censor books in schools and libraries, ban teaching about racial and sexual discrimination, and pass laws to empower mass lawsuits against public schools and universities for teaching about historical oppression. These laws employ different strategies to push a rightist cultural and political agenda: mass vigilante lawsuits, censorship, and requirements for ideological balance to "both sides" of every issue, including slavery and the Holocaust. These laws are aimed at, on the one hand, preventing the teaching of historical conflicts, oppression, and inequality, and, on the other hand, requiring the teaching of right-wing and Christian fundamentalist dogma and jingoistic patriotism.

Contradictorily, these laws are claiming that education is not political and hence punishing the teaching of knowledge about social injustice and then claiming that right-wing views must be included in the curriculum. The strategies employed in Texas and Florida to empower vigilante lawsuits by right-wing activists in the name of "parental rights" are not merely about waging war on educational approaches that would provide students with self and social understanding necessary for democratic governance. They are also part of a broader right-wing war on public institutions. The attack on public educational institutions needs to be comprehended in the context of the broader right-wing war on civil liberties, voting rights, the rights to free expression and public protest, and the effort to destroy public institutions that care for and support people. By late 2022, twenty-five states had passed sixty-four laws affecting 42 percent of the US population.[4] As *The Washington Post* reports,

> A plurality of the passed laws, 42 percent, bar transgender students from playing on sports teams that match their gender identities. . . . Laws limiting instruction on race, racism and history make up 28 percent of all passed laws. Legislation that restricts what teachers can discuss related to gender identity, sexuality and LGBTQ issues accounts for 23 percent of the passed laws.[5]

Right-wing populists such as Governor Ron Desantis of Florida appear confused about the politics of education. He has assailed critical race theory as if it is practiced in schools rather than recognizing that it is largely a higher education discourse originally developed in law schools. He also criticizes one resilience program, social and emotional learning, as bringing left-wing politics to the classroom. In fact, as prior chapters have detailed, it does no such thing. Social and emotional learning depoliticizes knowledge and curriculum and centers feelings, affect, learned self-control, and interpersonal communication. Right-wing populists perceive SEL as a liberal agenda and, in contrast, lay claim to a revival of a canon of jingoistic, nationalist, Eurocentric, and white supremacist curriculum and expression in schools while censoring other political views and claiming neutrality.

As discussed in prior chapters, the standards and accountability movement, which was deeply intertwined with the global corporate school reform movement, promoted high-stakes standardized testing and the standardization of curriculum. The standards and accountability movement revived the ideology of positivism suggesting that knowledge should be conceived as a collection of facts. In this view, the values, assumptions, and ideologies that undergird concepts and truth claims have no import. That is, citizens are being miseducated to see truth as a function of authority rather than interpreting claims to truth by the strength of argument and evidence and by situating claims to truth in relation to broader social, culture, and political structures and forces. This cultural crisis appears in the widespread susceptibility to conspiracy theory that provides simplistic, emotionally potent explanation and that mystifies social causes as the mysterious super-agency of vilified groups or strongmen.[6]

As distinct from the standards and accountability movement, resilience pedagogies such as social and emotional learning, grit, biometric pedagogy, meditation programs, and mindfulness programs seem to appeal to people by their attention to subjectivity—affect, behavior, emotions, desire, pleasure, cultural relevance, and so on. However, these resilience pedagogies, while seeming to break with radical objectivism, err by embracing a radical subjectivism. That is, students' feelings, emotions, and affect are taken up as being meaningful and valuable on their own without consideration for how subjective experience is socially formed by objective forces in the world. Yet, even as resilience programs seem to embrace radical subjectivism, multiple resilience programs have been developed particularly through digital technology as demanding supposed objective quantified measures. Social and emotional learning has been "objectivized" by the World Bank and the World Economic Forum. These supranational organizations have sought to transform affect and behavior into "objective" quantified measures by drawing on psychological categories that lend themselves to empirical data collection. As well, these organizations have been working with the Lego Foundation to quantify play and play-based learning and to make play into a quantifiable global learning standard. As Lego and other entertainment companies morph into education and edutainment companies, the quantification of affect and behavior stands to allow student activity to be translated into commercially valuable data that can be exchanged, used to create consumer profiles, and enhance marketing. Similarly, digital products including so-called Personalized Learning standardized curriculum products, AI reading avatars, digital SEL products, and digital surveillance apps all aspire to translate the bodily movements, behavior, and affect of children into data that is run through big data algorithms to sell a number of products to districts and parents. These products promise student resilience and self-control, learned efficacy, calm and mindfulness, lots of surveillance, and the sorting and sifting of students based on the data.

Resilience pedagogies and programs including digital products, for the most part, do not lend themselves to democratic education. These various practices of subjectivist programs of self-control, curricular standardization, techno-tracking, surveillance, and commercialism do not facilitate critical dialogue between teachers and students. They foster hierarchical social relations and aim to instill self-regulation in the interest of docility and knowledge consumption. Nor do they foster habits of critical engagement with knowledge and the conditions of its making. As well, resilience products take up student subjectivity in a way that is delinked from the broader social, political, cultural, and economic forces and structures that form the self and delink the self from the capacity of learning to impact the social world students inhabit. Consequently, resilience programs do not model democratic social relationships. Nor do they foster democratic social relations outside of schools.

Cultural politics refers to the struggle over knowledge and meanings. It relates broader social antagonisms among classes and cultural groups to the contests over meanings within educative institutions. Democratic forms of education make cultural politics central to pedagogy. For people to engage in civic life they need to understand the values, assumptions, ideologies, and interests underlying claims to truth. Public education has become increasingly dominated by commercial and instrumental approaches to pedagogy and curriculum. STEM and Career and Technical Education promote vocational and instrumental framings of subjects of study, schooling, and knowledge as in service to work, and they harness knowledge to its market uses rather than its civic potential. These curriculum movements have become the centerpiece of long-standing efforts to wrongly claim knowledge as not just apolitical, disinterested, and neutral but also as needing to be commercially valuable—a perspective that is hardly neutral and apolitical as it represents the worldviews and interests of owners of business. The false neutrality of these market perspectives actively denies the cultural politics of knowledge—that knowledge is contested and that those contests are tied to the material and symbolic interests and different groups and classes. Curriculum and pedagogical approaches that openly embrace cultural politics foster the critical engagement with knowledge and the relationships between knowledge and social authority. Democratic education that centralizes cultural politics stands to challenge material and symbolic inequality in its various forms by empowering individuals and groups to comprehend how knowledge-making relates to social power, the interests and ideological perspectives of classes and cultural groups. A number of educational traditions embrace cultural politics as a prerequisite for democratic educational practices including critical pedagogy, progressive education, culturally responsive pedagogy, critical race theory, and decolonial pedagogy.

The Displacement of Knowledge Traditions

In both K–12 and higher education a number of traditions of knowledge have been drastically reduced or eradicated from curricula. During the neoliberal restructuring of public and higher education, abstract subjects have been scaled back as allegedly practical and more directly commercially useful subjects have been maintained or expanded. Humanities and social science traditions have been reduced. Even abstract mathematics and abstract science have been scaled back in favor of applied mathematics, applied science, engineering, and technology. These trends have been evidenced in the Common Core State Standards, which were spearheaded by the Gates Foundation, in the near-universal adoption of STEM curricula, and in the wide embrace of Career and Technical Education. Under the Common Core in a particularly glaring example, literature has been often renamed "Language Arts" and reduced and replaced by the teaching of technical instructional repair manuals for appliances. There are a number of problems with the reduction of the humanities and social science traditions. These are traditions that (particularly when engaged critically rather than canonically) provide fertile ground for the development of imagination, the analysis of narrative, critical social faculties of interpretation and judgment, and the tools to comprehend the formation of subjectivity and consciousness in relation to social contexts. These are intellectual tools for participation in collective self-governance in a democratic society.

The humanities and social sciences do not guarantee a politics. For example, literature and philosophy can be taught canonically as "great works" that are the inheritance of "the best and the brightest." Such a dogmatic approach tends to discourage the critical engagement with the work and shuts down questions about the values and interests animating a narrative and how that narrative asks readers in a contemporary setting to make particular identifications. As sociologist Stanley Aronowitz has pointed out in *Against Schooling and for an Education that Matters*, historically works of literature and philosophy were read in factories and collectively discussed by workers as they were working.[7] Literature provides not just entertaining stories and glimpses into the consciousness of a character and a time period and social dynamics. It provides ways of imagining the world differently than it is. Philosophy provides not just a history of concepts that inform practices in the present and solutions to problems but ways of taking apart and rethinking the framing of problems themselves, not to mention a legacy of ethical thought. These traditions are indispensable to a self-reflective society, a society with a conscience, and a society committed to democracy.

Resilience programs do not provide students with the intellectual tools, scholarly traditions, or theories of self and society to foster in students' knowledge and dispositions for collective democratic self-governance. Resilience programs neither model democracy nor provide the intellectual and critical concepts and dispositions for democracy outside of schools.

Bowles and Gintis, in their classic book *Schooling in Capitalist America*, discuss how the historical expansion of higher education access to working-class youth post–Second World War resulted in these youth studying the humanities and social sciences.[8] These traditions of knowledge opened up questions about the society and the self in these students that contributed to the development of a more reflective and socially critical citizenry. This was a factor in the development of a number of social movements in the postwar era, including civil rights, the women's movement, gay rights, labor movement, antiwar, ecological, and other movements. These movements were united by an aspiration for equality, freedom from domination, and a recognition that social struggles shared a common emancipatory aspiration.

Unfortunately, such universal democratic aspirations, cultivated through education and unifying different struggles against oppression, are being threatened by sectarian politics grounded in essentialism.

Resurgent Racial Essentialism, Identity Politics, and Resilience

Racial essentialism is the belief that physical racial characteristics guarantee the views, ideologies, and values of individuals and groups. Pernicious rightist ideologies, including white supremacy and eugenics, are grounded in racial essentialism. Right-wing populism, rightist nationalism, and Trumpism have fueled white supremacy to scapegoat racial and ethnic minorities for the social maladies that their policies have produced—poverty, unemployment, inequality, and migration have resulted from neoliberal capitalism.

Racial essentialism has recently found adherents among some identity politics-oriented liberals who equate white identity and whiteness with oppression rather than distinguishing between whiteness as an identity position and white supremacy as an oppressive racial ideology. Racial essentialism presumes a conception of community in which social hierarchy and inequality is a natural consequence of the nature of races of people rather than comprehending hierarchy and inequality as a historical and contingent, yet changeable, outcome. White supremacists view the material and symbolic power of whiteness as deserved, due to inherent superiority, and under threat. Essentialist identity politics liberals view white privilege and economic and cultural power as proof of the evilness of white people. In this view, the only thing white people can do about racism is feel guilt and shame for their identity position and maybe spread guilt and shame to other white people. This view typically also positions racism as a permanent feature of society (rather than a pedagogical project that can be eradicated with other pedagogical projects), thereby suturing to racial essentialism, permanent white guilt and non-white permanent victimhood, the impossibility of collective struggle. In place of collective anti-racist struggle, people get trainings in work and school that promote these views as anti-racism.[9] Not only is this bad anti-racist politics, in that it forecloses the possibility of anti-racist white alliance and struggle, but it also fuels white supremacists by affirming their assumptions of racial defensiveness. In fact, white identity can be anti-essentialist, recognizing that race is a social construction and it can be defined by anti-racism and universal solidarity as well as the development of anti-racist pedagogies.

White supremacists are deeply antidemocratic for their views against racial and other forms of equality as well as for their hatred of open public discourse and desire to dominate public discourse. In education, this is evident in widespread efforts to censor books and curricula that do not accord with their view. Racial essentialist identity politics liberals also tend to be antidemocratic for their willingness to shut down public discourse.

Resilience projects, rather than providing the means to challenge racial essentialism, white supremacist ideology, and other antidemocratic ideologies, falsely purport to be apolitical efficacy tools for transmission of knowledge. Resilience projects consequently ask teachers and students not to comprehend knowledge in relation to broader social forces and cultural and class antagonisms that produce the very racism that many students and others experience. Instead, by grounding projects in emotional tropes of trauma, resilience psychologizes the political. What is more, resilience projects of learned self-regulation and control, like privatization schemes, disproportionately target working-class and poor Black and Brown students. Subjectivist resilience projects disarm these students of the tools to make sense of and counter the racialized class violence they experience.

Hence, despite the rhetoric of being "culturally sensitive," resilience projects provide no intellectual tools such as social theory or dialogic exchange that take up students' cultures and experiences in relation to power, politics, history, or ethics. In the face of expanding white supremacist movements, xenophobia, anti-Muslim and anti-Jewish hate, students in resilience programs are being taught to turn inward and focus only on themselves and their feelings and their self-control and turn away from the monumental changes in the world that threaten them and others. They are being asked to focus on their own bodies but not in ways that help them understand how their bodies are discursively constructed in ways that suture racial ideologies to the body. Whereas anti-racist pedagogies denaturalize and challenge essentialist claims about race, resilience pedagogies refuse to recognize race and racism, not to mention cultural politics itself—the ways contested meanings are part of broader class and cultural group antagonisms. The point not to be missed here is that resilience pedagogies are at odds with approaches to education that help students comprehend social tendencies, social antagonisms, and pressing public problems such that they can act as citizens with others to address them. This is the case whether the public problem is the current crises of democracy, racism, global warming and environmental disaster, or worsening economic inequality and poverty.

Notes

Chapter 1

1 Kathleen Tierney, *The Social Roots of Risk: Producing Disasters, Promoting Resilience* (Stanford: Stanford University Press, 2014), 6.

2 Paulo Freire, *Pedagogy of the Oppressed* (New York: Continuum, 1972).

3 See for example, Brad Evans and Julian Reid, *Resilient Life: The Art of Living Dangerously* (Malden, MA: Polity Press, 2014); David Chandler and Julian Reid, *The Neoliberal Subject: Resilience, Adaptation, and Vulnerability* (New York: Rowman & Littlefield, 2016).

4 I make this point in relation to grit in Kenneth J. Saltman, *Scripted Bodies: Corporate Power, Smart Technologies, and the Undoing of Public Education* (New York: Routledge, 2016). See an excellent chapter on resilience that makes this point: Graham B. Slater, "The Precarious Subject of Neoliberal Education: Resilient Life in the Catastrophic Conjuncture," in *Handbook of Critical Approaches to Politics and Policy of Education*, eds. Kenneth J. Saltman and Nicole Nguyen (New York: Routledge, 2022).

5 Ulrich Beck, *Risk Society: Towards a New Modernity* (Thousand Oaks: Sage, 1992).

6 Zygmunt Bauman, *In Search of Politics* (Stanford: Stanford University Press, 1999).

7 See Nancy Fraser, "From Discipline to Flexibilization: Rereading Foucault in the Shadow of Globalization," *Constellations* 10, no. 2 (2003): 160–71; Angela McRobbie, "Top Girls?," *Cultural Studies* 21, no. 4–5 (2007): 718–37.

8 Nancy Fraser, *Cannibal Capitalism* (New York: Verso, 2022).

9 Fraser, *Cannibal Capitalism*. While Fraser emphasizes how capitalism cannibalizes schools as institutions of care and responsibility, we can add to this that it cannibalizes institutions capable of fostering critical consciousness shutting them down as sites and stakes of struggle.

10 "Cultural pedagogy" is a term that was significantly developed by Henry Giroux. Part of the value of the term is that it emphasizes the educative dimensions of culture through ideology or discourse. Since everyone is

implicated in culture, that is, meaning-making practice, and culture is educative, this term highlights the extent to which people's signifying practices matter politically by informing shared understandings, language, and the knowledge and discursive inventories from which people form their identities. See, for example, Henry A. Giroux, *Border Crossings*, 2nd Edition (New York: Routledge, 2005).

11 Two recent manifestos that make the case for an alternative include Fraser, *Cannibal Capitalism* and Chantal Mouffe, *Toward a Green Democratic Revolution* (New York: Verso, 2022).

12 Resilience programs nearly universally have meaningless content because they fail to take up subjects either in relation to the broader social world that gives meaning to the subjects or in relation to student experiences and cultures. Nonetheless resilience programs frequently employ doublespeak by naming standardized and test-oriented programs "personalized."

13 Some of my own critical scholarship on the neoliberal restructuring of public education includes Kenneth J. Saltman, *Collateral Damage: Corporatizing Schools— A Threat to Democracy* (Lanham, MD: Rowman & Littlefield, 2000); Robin Truth Goodman and Kenneth J. Saltman, *Strange Love: Or How We Learn to Stop Worrying and Love the Market* (Lanham, MD: Rowman & Littlefield, 2002); Kenneth J. Saltman, *The Edison Schools* (New York: Routledge, 2005); Kenneth J. Saltman, *Capitalizing on Disaster: Taking and Breaking Public Schools* (New York: Routledge, 2007); Kenneth J. Saltman, *The Gift of Education: Public Education and Venture Philanthropy* (New York: Palgrave, 2010); Kenneth J. Saltman, *The Failure of Corporate School Reform* (New York: Routledge, 2012); Saltman, *Scripted Bodies*; Kenneth J. Saltman, *The Swindle of Innovative Educational Finance* (Minneapolis: University of Minnesota Press, 2018); Kenneth J. Saltman, *The Alienation of Fact: AI, Digital Educational Privatization and the False Promise of Bodies and Numbers* (Cambridge: MIT Press, 2022).

14 See David Hursh, *High Stakes Testing and the Decline of Teaching and Learning* (Lanham, MD: Rowman & Littlefield, 2008); David Hursh, *The End of Public Schools: The Corporate Reform Agenda to Privatize Education* (New York: Routledge, 2015).

15 Freire, *Pedagogy of the Oppressed* used this expression "the ones who know" to describe the transmission model of pedagogy or the mistaken

concept of depositing knowledge as "banking education." Historically, this conception of the student as empty vessel to be filled (or, same concept, different metaphor, a "blank slate" to be written upon) traces back to philosophical empiricism typified by John Locke, *An Essay Concerning Human Understanding* (1690; Oxford: Oxford University Press, 1798) and Jean Jacques Rousseau, *Emile, or on Education* (1763; New York: Basic Books, 1979) in the Western Enlightenment tradition.

16 Christopher Robbins, *Expelling Hope: The Assault on Youth and the Militarization of Schooling* (Albany: SUNY Press, 2009); Kenneth J. Saltman and David Gabbard, eds., *Education as Enforcement: The Militarization and Corporatization of Schools*, Second Edition (2002; New York: Routledge, 2010).

17 See the work of Pasi Sahlberg, Antoni Verger, and Susan Robertson among others on G.E.R.M.

18 David Hursh, Jeanette Deutermann, Lisa Rudley, Zhe Chen, and Sarah McGinnis, *Opting Out: The Story of the Parents' Grassroot Movement to Achieve Whole Child Public Schools* (Gorham, ME: Meyers Educational Press, 2020).

19 Around 2010 at the peak of the corporate school reform push for privatization, liberal critics of educational privatization managed to get public attention for their criticisms. Most notable was former privatization advocate and Republican assistant secretary of education Diane Ravitch. The long-standing left critics of privatization who had for decades related educational privatization to broader political-economic, cultural politics, and global structural forces and antagonisms were ignored as liberal, ideologically acceptable framings dominated the counter position to privatization in public discourse. These liberals framed the issue not in terms of neoliberal policy and ideology but narrowly in terms of defending public schools, efficacious service delivery, a "strong curriculum," all along denying the politics of knowledge and curriculum.

20 I detail the evidence in Saltman, *The Failure of Corporate School Reform*.

21 Martin Carnoy, "School Vouchers Are Not a Proven Strategy for Improving Student Achievement," *Economic Policy Institute,* February 28, 2017, available at http://www.epi.org/publication/school-vouchers-are-not-a-proven-strategy-for-improving-student-achievement/; Kevin Welner, *Neovouchers: The Emergence of Tuition Tax Credits for Private Schooling* (Lanham, MD: Rowman & Littlefield, 2008).

22 Tomas Monarrez, Brian Kisida, and Matthew M. Chingos, "The Effect of Charter Schools on School Segregation," *EdWorkingPaper* 20-308, 2020, retrieved December 11, 2022, from Annenberg Institute at Brown University, https://doi.org/10.26300/1z61-br35.

23 The Chicago Teachers Union's Caucus of Rank and File Educators CORE under the leadership of Karen Lewis, Jesse Sharkey, and Stacy Davis Gates expanded the union's focus to poverty, privatization, venture philanthropy, racism, and other broad social issues imbricated with teacher labor.

24 See Milton Friedman, *Capitalism and Freedom* (Chicago: University of Chicago Press, 1962), for an early argument for shifting public education to markets. Gary Becker, *Human Capital* (Chicago: University of Chicago Press, 1964).

25 The assumptions of human capital theory in education can be seen, for example, in the scholarship of Eric Hanushek, a fellow of the Hoover Institution.

26 Liberal social democratic remedies for poverty such as redistribution, authoritative public program expansion, and progressive taxation can be found advocated by, for example, Thomas Piketty or in education in the work of Jean Anyon, *Radical Possibilities* (New York: Routledge, 2005). The project to address poverty and inequality by democratizing the ownership and control over capital can be found elaborated in the work of Richard Wolff and Michael Albert, among others. See, for example, Richard D. Wolff and Stephen A. Resnick, *Contending Economic Theories: Neoclassical, Keynesian, and Marxian* (Cambridge: MIT Press, 2015). Wolff in many places makes the case that far from being utopian there are many actually existing economic models in which workers play a managerial role and the divide between ownership and value creation is not split. See his film about the 2008 financial crisis, *Capitalism Hits the Fan.*

27 David Harvey, *A Brief History of Neoliberalism* (Oxford: Oxford University Press, 2007).

28 See, for example, Joel Spring, *The Economization of Education: Human Capital, Global Corporations, Skills-Based Schooling* (New York: Routledge, 2015).

29 Stephanie Black's documentary film *Life and Debt* (2001) clearly illustrates this example of Jamaica under neoliberal structural adjustment. The

film includes coverage of the Kingston Tax Free Zone. I witnessed the same super-exploitation in the Montego Tax Free Zone, in which both manufacturing and intellectual labor were being done at miniscule pay by university-educated workers with the government receiving no taxes from the corporations benefiting from the labor.

30 Fraser, *Cannibal Capitalism*.

31 William I. Robinson, *Into the Tempest* (Chicago: Haymarket, 2019).

32 William I. Robinson, *The Global Police State* (London: Pluto Press, 2020).

33 Fraser, *Cannibal Capitalism*; Harvey, *A Brief History of Neoliberalism*; Michael Perelman, *The Invention of Capitalism* (Durham: Duke University Press, 2000).

34 Nick Couldry and Ulises A. Mejias, *The Costs of Connection: How Data Is Colonizing Human Life and Appropriating It for Capitalism* (Stanford: Stanford University Press, 2019).

35 See Samuel Bowles and Herbert Gintis, *Schooling in Capitalist America* (1976; Chicago: Haymarket, 2011); Pierre Bourdieu and Jean Passeron, *Social and Cultural Reproduction in Education* (Thousand Oaks: Sage, 1992); Louis Althusser, "Ideology and Ideological State Apparatuses: Notes Toward an Investigation," in *Lenin and Philosophy and Other Essays* (New York: Monthly Review Press, 2001), 85–126; for theories that draw on, complicate, and challenge aspects of reproduction theories in education, see Michael Apple, *Ideology and Curriculum* (New York: Routledge, 1977) and Henry A. Giroux, *Theory and Resistance in Education* (Westport: Bergin & Garvey, 1983).

36 Fraser, "From Discipline to Flexibilization."

37 McRobbie, "Top Girls?" 718–37.

Chapter 2

1 Kenneth J. Saltman and David Gabbard, eds., *Education as Enforcement: The Militarization and Corporatization of Schools* (New York: Routledge, 2002).

2 Saltman and Gabbard, *Education as Enforcement*.

3 ADHD diagnoses and prescriptions exploded with the advent of high-stakes standardized testing at the start of the 2000s. I discuss this in

"Chapter One: Smart Drugs: Corporate Profit and Corporeal Control" in Saltman, *Scripted Bodies.*

4	I take this up in Saltman, *The Alienation of Fact.*

5	Antonio Gramsci, *Selections from the Prison Notebooks*, ed. Quinton Hoare (New York: International Publishers, 1971), 3–23. Gramsci explains that the traditional intellectuals elaborate ideological common sense on behalf of the ruling class but that "One of the most important characteristics of any group that is developing toward dominance is its struggle to assimilate and conquer 'ideologically' the traditional intellectuals, but this assimilation and conquest is made quicker and more efficacious the more the group in question succeeds in simultaneously elaborating its own organic intellectuals" (10). Resilience discourse is an ideological product of the traditional intellectuals. Critical pedagogy represents the possibility of ideological conquest toward a radically democratic hegemony. See the work of Chantal Mouffe and Henry Giroux.

6	Indeed, this is the accusation waged by right-wing populists who contend that the focus on feelings, say in social and emotional learning, detracts from the delivery of what they deem worthwhile knowledge—instrumental and commercially oriented training in skills paired with Eurocentric and even white nationalist cultural agenda. They accuse SEL of being a radical leftist agenda. In reality, SEL suffers from delinking subjective feelings from the objective structures and forces that produce feelings and contexts that inform feelings. SEL largely fails to recognize the dialectical interplay of subjectivity and objectivity as proponents call for attention to emotions to be a technique in facilitating transmission models of pedagogy, what Freire called Banking Education. The subjectivism of SEL accords more with liberal views that inflate subjective autonomy and delimit the role of structural forces in the formation of subjectivity.

7	In *Lectures on Negative Dialectics* Theodor Adorno writes, "Human beings are in fact zoon politikon, 'political animals', in the sense that they can only survive by virtue of society and social institutions to which, as autonomous and critical subjectivity, they stand opposed. . . . So what I am saying is that he [Hegel] destroyed the illusion of the subject's being-in-itself and showed that the subject is itself an aspect of social objectivity" (16).

8 Ben Williamson and Nelli Piattoeva, "Objectivity as Standardization in Data-scientific Education Policy, Technology, and Governance," *Learning, Media and Technology* 44 (2019): 64–76.

9 https://casel.org/fundamentals-of-sel/.

10 Chandler and Reid, *The Neoliberal Subject*, 4.

11 I discuss this in Saltman, *Scripted Bodies*. See also Ben Williamson, *Big Data in Education* (Thousand Oaks: Sage, 2017).

12 Glenda Kwek, "Brains and Bracelets: Gates Funds Wrist Sensors for Students," *The Sydney Morning Herald*, June 14, 2012.

13 I detail CZI's Summit personalized learning platform in Saltman, *The Swindle of Innovative Educational Finance*. See Faith Boninger, Alex Molnar, and C. Saldana, "Personalized Learning and the Digital Privatization of Curriculum and Teaching," *National Education Policy Center* (April 2019), retrieved February 3, 2020, from http://nepc.colorado .edu/publication/personalized-learning.

14 Chandler and Reid, *The Neoliberal Subject*, 1–2 & 76.

15 Paul Tough, *How Children Succeed: Grit, Curiosity, and the Hidden Power of Character* (New York: Houghton-Mifflin, 2012).

16 Angela Duckworth TED Talk, "Grit: The Power of Passion and Perseverance," May 9, 2013, https://www.ted.com/talks/angela_lee _duckworth_grit_the_power_of passion_and_perseverance?language=en See also her account in Tough, *How Children Succeed*.

17 Freire, *Pedagogy of the Oppressed*.

18 Kenneth J. Saltman, "The Austerity School: Grit, Character, and the Privatization of Education," *Symploke* 22, no. 1–2 (2014): 41–57.

19 Retrieved June 3, 2022, from https://www.davidlynchfoundation.org/ about-us.html.

20 Alexander Means, *Schooling in the Age of Austerity* (New York: Palgrave Macmillan, 2013).

21 https://calmclassroom.com.

22 This is a point stressed by critical sociologist Pierre Bourdieu. See for example Bourdieu and Passeron, *Social and Cultural Reproduction in Education*. See also the documentary on Bourdieu by Pierre Carles, *Sociology Is a Martial Art* (2001).

23 The measurement of "non-cognitive skills" and claims to expanding them in the interest of transmissional models of schooling are being promoted

hy human capital advocates like James Heckman. For an important
analysis of how supranational organizations are objectivizing behavior
and affect, see Williamson and Piattoeva, "Objectivity as Standardization"
64–76.

24 See, for example, World Economic Forum, "Schools of the Future:
Defining New Models of Education for the Fourth Industrial Revolution"
(January, 2020); OECD, "Skills for Social Progress" (March 10, 2015),
https://doi.org/10.1787/23078731; Rachel Parker and Bo Stjerne
Thomsen, "Executive Summary: Learning Through Play at School," White
Paper Lego Foundation (March 2019); Ben Mandell, Daniel Wilson,
Jen Ryan, Katie Ertel, Mara Drechevsky, and Megina Baker, "Towards
a Pedagogy of Play: A Project Zero Working Paper" (July 2016); The
Lego Foundation, "Assessing Creativity: A Palette of Possibilities"; The
Pedagogy of Play Research Team, "Playful Participatory Research: An
Emerging Methodology for Developing a Pedagogy of Play" A Project
Zero Working Paper [Project Zero at Harvard Graduate School of
Education/International School at Billund Funded by Lego Foundation]
(July 2016); The Lego Foundation, "What We Mean by: Creativity"];
The Lego Foundation, "Creating Systems: How Can Education Systems
Reform to Enhance Learners' Creativity?" Creativity Matters No. 2;
Bonnie Cramond, "Appendix: Choosing a Creativity Assessment That is
Fit For Purpose," The Lego Foundation.

25 Parker and Thomsen, "Executive Summary: Learning Through Play
at School"; Mandell et al., "Towards a Pedagogy of Play"; The Lego
Foundation, "Assessing Creativity: A Palette of Possibilities"; The
Pedagogy of Play Research Team, "Playful Participatory Research: An
Emerging Methodology for Developing a Pedagogy of Play"; The Lego
Foundation, "What We Mean by: Creativity"; The Lego Foundation,
"Creating Systems: How Can Education Systems Reform to Enhance
Learners' Creativity?"; Cramond, "Appendix: Choosing a Creativity
Assessment That is Fit For Purpose."

26 Jathan Sadowski, "When Data Is Capital: Datafication, Accumulation, and
Extraction," *Big Data and Society* 6 (January-June 2019): 1–12.

27 The scholarship of James Heckman typifies this view. For criticism of
human capital discourse in education see Spring, *The Economization of
Education*.

28 Chandler and Reid, *The Neoliberal Subject*, 94.

29 Parker and Thomsen, "Executive Summary: Learning through Play," 1 and 9.

30 Diane Levin makes this argument in the documentary *Mickey Mouse Monopoly* (2002) produced by Media Education Foundation. It can be found in the transcript on page 17. Transcript available at https://www.mediaed.org/transcripts/Mickey-Mouse-Monopoly-Transcript.pdf.

31 Lego's project of supplying children with premade corporate narrative derived from Hollywood movies and mass-marketed video games ought to be scrutinized not only for providing prefabricated stories but for the kinds of ideologies, values, and identifications supplied to children that form the building blocks of their narratives and play. Such largely conservatizing commercial ideologies need to be understood in contrast to other more emancipatory ideologies, values, and identifications that accord with broader ethical and political values of equality, democracy, and justice. For criticism of the corporatization of children's culture and better ideological alternatives, see Henry Giroux, *The Mouse that Roared: Disney and the End of Innocence* (Lanham: MD: Rowman & Littlefield, 1999).

32 Gregory Schmidt, "Lego Builds an Empire Brick by Brick," *The New York Times*, February 14, 2014, B1.

33 The Lego Foundation's reports and advocacy materials make these aims explicit and the OECD's reports include the play-based learning agenda as part of its neoliberal human capital development perspective. See, for example, Parker and Thomsen, "Executive Summary: Learning Through Play"; Mandell et al., "Towards a Pedagogy of Play"; The Lego Foundation, "Assessing Creativity: A Palette of Possibilities"; The Pedagogy of Play Research Team, "Playful Participatory Research: An Emerging Methodology for Developing a Pedagogy of Play"; The Lego Foundation, "What We Mean By: Creativity"; The Lego Foundation, "Creating Systems: How Can Education Systems Reform to Enhance Learners' Creativity?"; Cramond, "Appendix: Choosing a Creativity Assessment That Is Fit for Purpose."

34 On the discourse of childhood innocence and its political and pedagogical dimensions see Giroux, *The Mouse That Roared*, and Henry A. Giroux, *Stealing Innocence: Youth, Corporate Power, and the Politics of Culture* (New York: Palgrave Macmillan, 2000).

35 See Alexander J. Means, *Learning to Save the Future* (New York: Routledge, 2018). See also Nick Dyer-Witheford, Atle Mikkola Kjosen, and James Steinhoff, *Inhuman Power: Artificial Intelligence and the Future of Capitalism* (London: Pluto Press, 2019).

36 Williamson and Piattoeva, "Objectivity as Standardization."

37 Williamson and Piattoeva, "Objectivity as Standardization," 10.

38 Williamson and Piattoeva, "Objectivity as Standardization," 9.

39 Williamson and Piattoeva, "Objectivity as Standardization," 11.

40 OECD, "Social and Emotional Skills: Well-Being, Connectedness, and Success"; World Economic Forum, "Schools of the Future: Defining New Models of Education for the Fourth Industrial Revolution," 1–33. www .weforum.org.

41 See World Economic Forum, "Schools of the Future: Defining New Models of Education for the Fourth Industrial Revolution," 11, 13, 26.

42 Williamson and Piattoeva, "Objectivity as Standardization," 14; Saltman, *Scripted Bodies.*

43 See Alysson McDowell's blog Wrench in the Gears. Wrench in the Gears (blog). https://wrenchinthegears.com.

44 World Economic Forum, "Schools of the Future: Defining New Models of Education for the Fourth Industrial Revolution," 7.

45 World Economic Forum, "Schools of the Future: Defining New Models of Education for the Fourth Industrial Revolution," 4.

46 Freire, *Pedagogy of the Oppressed*; Donaldo Macedo, *Literacies of Power* (New York: Westview, 2006).

47 World Economic Forum, "Schools of the Future: Defining New Models of Education for the Fourth Industrial Revolution," 9.

48 Henry Giroux, *On Critical Pedagogy*, 2nd Edition (New York: Bloomsbury, 2020).

49 Giroux, *On Critical Pedagogy.*

Chapter 3

1 Saltman, *Capitalizing on Disaster*; Kenneth J. Saltman, *Schooling in Disaster Capitalism* (New York: Routledge, 2007).

2	Intergovernmental Panel on Climate Change [IPCC], "Summary for Policymakers," in *Climate Change 2021: The Physical Science Basis. Contribution of Working Group I to the Sixth Assessment Report of the Intergovernmental Panel on Climate Change*, eds. V. Masson- Delmotte, P. Zhai, A. Pirani, S.L. Connors, C. Péan, S. Berger, N. Caud, Y. Chen, L. Goldfarb, M.I. Gomis, M. Huang, K. Leitzell, E. Lonnoy, J. B. R. Matthews, T. K. Maycock, T. Waterfield, O. Yelekçi, R. Yu and B. Zhou (Cambridge: Cambridge University Press, 2021), In Press, 1–31; The Federal Emergency Management Agency provides data on present and historical disruptive storms. See https://www.fema.gov/disaster/historic.

3	Intergovernmental Panel on Climate Change [IPCC], "Summary for Policymakers."

4	Intergovernmental Panel on Climate Change [IPCC], "Summary for Policymakers."

5	World Economic Forum, "The Global Risks Report 2021" (2021), retrieved September 27, 2021, from http://www3.weforum.org/docs/WEF_The_Global_Risks_Report_2021.pdf.

6	Saltman, *Capitalizing on Disaster;* Saltman, *Schooling in Disaster Capitalism.*

7	Thomas C. Pedroni, "Through Jean Anyon's 'Screen Door': The Differentially Racialized Incursion of the Neoliberal State in Milwaukee and Detroit Schools," *Teachers College Record* 123, no. 14 (2021): 115–28.

8	P. Mirowski, *Never Let a Serious Crisis Go to Waste* (New York: Verso, 2014); Naomi Klein, *The Shock Doctrine* (New York: Metropolitan Books, 2007); Saltman, *Capitalizing on Disaster;* Saltman, *Schooling in Disaster Capitalism.*

9	The National Security Strategy of the United States of America (2002 September), retrieved September 27, 2021, from https://georgewbush-whitehouse.archives.gov/nsc/nss/2002/.

10	Intergovernmental Panel on Climate Change [IPCC], "Summary for Policymakers."

11	J. Tollefson, "Why Deforestation and Extinction Make Pandemics More Likely," *Nature*, August 7, 2020, retrieved September 27, 2021, from https://www.nature.com/articles/d41586-020-02341-1.

12	Ben Williamson, R. Eynon, and J. Potter, "Pandemic Politics, Pedagogies and Practices: Digital Technologies and Distance Education During the Coronavirus Emergency," *Learning, Media and Technology* 45, no. 2 (2020): 107–14, https://doi.org/10.1080/17439884.2020.1761641.

13 Education Week, "The Coronavirus Spring: The Historic Closing of U.S. Schools (A Timeline)," July 1, 2020, retrieved December 14, 2021, https:// www.edweek.org/leadership/the-coronavirus-spring-the-historic-closing -of-u-s-schools-a-timeline/2020/07.

14 Frank Catalano, "Pandemic Spurs Changes in the Edtech Schools Use, from the Classroom to the Admin Office," *EdSurge*, January 26, 2021, retrieved December 13, 2021, from https://www.edsurge.com/news/2021 -01-26-pandemic-spurs-changes-in-the-edtech-schools-use-from-the -classroom-to-the-admin-office.

15 United States Department of Education Office of Civil Rights, "Education in a Pandemic: The Disparate Impact of Covid-19 on America's Students," retrieved December 14, 2021, from https://www2.ed.gov/about/offices/list /ocr/docs/20210608-impacts-of-covid19.pdf.

16 See the American Academy of Pediatrics website healthychildren.or g, "Where We Stand: Screen Time," retrieved December 14, 2021, from https://www.healthychildren.org/English/family-life/Media/Pages/Where -We-Stand-TV-Viewing-Time.aspx?_gl=1*152d12x*_ga*ODU0NzUxMD A0LjE2Mzk1MDE3MjI.*_ga_FD9D3XZVQQ*MTYzOTUwMTcyMS4xLj EuMTYzOTUwMTk1My4w&_ga=2.131480847.1074417706.1639501722- 854751004.1639501722.

17 David K. Li, "Youth Suicide Attempts Soared During Pandemic, CDC Report Says," *NBC News*, June 11, 2021; Marie-Laure Charpignon, Johnattan Ontiveros, Saahil Sundaresan, Anika Puri, Jay Chandra, Kenneth D. Mandl, and Maimuna Shahnaz Majumder, "Evaluation of Suicides Among US Adolescents During the Covid-19 Pandemic," *JAMA Network* 176, no. 7 (2022): 724–6.

18 K. Mcelrath, "Nearly 93% of Households With School-Age Children Report Some Form of Distance Learning During Covid-19," August 20, 2020 census.gov retrieved December 14, 2021, from https://www.census.gov /library/stories/2020/08/schooling-during-the-covid-19-pandemic.html; United States Department of Education Office of Civil Rights, "Education in a Pandemic: The Disparate Impact of Covid-19 on America's Students."

19 Ben Williamson and Anna Hogan, "The Edtech Pandemic Shock," *Education International*, July 10, 2020 retrieved December 15, 2021, from

https://www.ei-ie.org/en/item/23423:the-edtech-pandemic-shock-by-ben
-williamson-anna-hogan.

20 J.P. Bailey, F.M. Hess, C. Cerf, C. Conaway, S. El-Mekki, D. Erquiaga, K.
Henderson, D. Klussmann, W. Lewis, P. Lockett, C. McQueen, K. Rausch,
N. Rees, G. Robinson, A. Rotherham, I. Rowe, I. Scott, H. Skandera, D.
Steiner, J. Weiss, and J. John White, "A Blueprint for Back to School,"
American Enterprise Institute, May 4, 2020, retrieved September 27, 2021,
from https://www.aei.org/research-products/report/a-blueprint-for-back
-to-school/; J. Bedrick and M. Ladner, "Let's Get Small: Microschools,
Pandemic Pods, and the Future of Education in America," The Heritage
Foundation Center for Education Policy No. 3540, October 6, 2020,
retrieved September 27, 2021, from https://www.heritage.org/education
/report/lets-get-small-microschools-pandemic-pods-and-the-future
-education-america.

21 On Cuomo's history of promoting public school privatization see Hursh,
The End of Public Schools. On Gates' privatization activities see Saltman,
The Gift of Education and Philip Kovacs, ed. *The Gates Foundation and the
Future of U.S. Public Schools* (New York: Routledge, 2011).

22 Valerie Strauss, "Cuomo Questions Why School Buildings Still Exist –
And Says New York Will Work with Bill Gates to 'Reimagine Education,'"
The Washington Post, May 6, 2020.

23 Kenneth J. Saltman, "Corporate Schooling Meets Corporate Media:
Standards, Testing, and Technophilia," *Review of Education Pedagogy
Cultural Studies* 38, no. 2 (2016): 105–23.

24 Saltman, "Corporate Schooling Meets Corporate Media."

25 Valerie Strauss, "Big Education Firms Spend Millions Lobbying for Pro-
Testing Policies," *Washington Post*, March 30, 2015.

26 Saltman, *The Swindle of Innovative Educational Finance*.

27 Mirowski, *Never Let a Serious Crisis Go to Waste*; Klein, *The Shock
Doctrine*; Saltman, *Capitalizing on Disaster*; Saltman, *Schooling in Disaster
Capitalism*; Naomi Klein, *The Battle for Paradise* (Chicago: Haymarket
Books, 2018). See the work of Thomas Pedroni and Henry Giroux on
Detroit, and Kristen Buras on post-Katrina New Orleans.

28 In New Orleans following Hurricane Katrina, a council of businesspeople,
the Bring New Orleans Back Commission (BNOB), refused to reopen or
rebuild the New Orleans public schools to instead establish four charter

school networks, fire all the public school teachers, and destroy the teacher's union.

29 Saltman, *Capitalizing on Disaster.*

30 Kenneth J. Saltman, "Chapter 1: Silver Linings and Golden Opportunities: The Corporate Plunder of Public Schools in Post-Katrina New Orleans," in *Capitalizing on Disaster.*

31 Saltman, *Capitalizing on Disaster.*

32 FEMA Crisis response and disaster resilience 2030: forging strategic response in an age of uncertainty (January 2012), 14

> **3. Infuse emergency management principles and life skills across the entire educational experience to empower individuals to assume more responsibility.** This means continuing to build emergency management awareness, from K through 12, with community-tailored curricula shaped by the local environment. It is about communicating the importance of partnering with individuals and community organizations to build self-reliance and individual initiative.
>
> *Why this need?* Future operating environments may well be characterized by significant decline in governmental resources for emergency management. Such fiscal constraints could tempt emergency managers to pull back from community engagement, which would widen the gap that already exists. Instead, it will be important to use the fiscal environment as an opportunity to reinvent and innovate. Schools and youth programs will be critically important channels, especially in creating awareness of new and unfamiliar threats such as pandemics or cyber attacks.

33 A. Molnar, Ed., G. Miron, M.K. Barbour, L. Huerta, S.R. Shafer, J.K. Rice, A. Glover, N. Browning, S. Hagle, and F. Boninger, *Virtual Schools in the U.S. 2021* (Boulder, CO: National Education Policy Center, 2021), retrieved September 29, 2021, from http://nepc.colorado.edu/publication/virtual-schools-annual-2021.

34 Gerald Bracey, "Knowledge Universe and Virtual Schools: Educational Breakthrough or Digital Raid on the Public Treasury?" Education Policy Studies Laboratory 2004, https://nepc.colorado.edu/publication/knowledge-universe-and-virtual-schools-educational-breakthrough-or-digital-raid-public-t; S. Butrymowicz, "Education Companies See an 'Upside to the Pandemic' for Business," *Hechinger Report* (June 18, 2020).

35 Molnar et al., *Virtual Schools in the U.S. 2021*, 4.

36 Boninger et al., "Personalized Learning and the Digital Privatization of Curriculum and Teaching," retrieved February 3, 2020, from http://nepc .colorado.edu/publication/personalized-learning.

37 Kenneth J. Saltman, *The Politics of Education: A Critical Introduction*, second Edition (New York: Routledge, 2018).

38 Saltman, *The Swindle of Innovative Educational Finance*.

39 Ben Williamson, F. Macgilchrist, and J. Potter, "Covid-19 Controversies and Critical Research in Digital Education," *Learning, Media and Technology* 46, no. 2 (2021): 117–27, https://doi.org/10.1080/17439884 .2021.1922437.

40 Molnar et al., *Virtual Schools in the U.S. 2021*.

41 Bailey et al., "A Blueprint for Back to School"; M. B. Horn, "The Rapid Rise of Pandemic Pods," *Education Next* 21, no. 1 (2021): 3, retrieved September 27, 2021, from https://www.educationnext.org/rapid-rise -pandemic-pods-will-parent-response-covid-19-lead-to-lasting-changes/; Bedrick and Ladner, "Let's Get Small: Microschools, Pandemic Pods, and the Future of Education in America."

42 Bailey et al., "A Blueprint for Back to School"; Bedrick and Ladner, "Let's Get Small: Microschools, Pandemic Pods, and the Future of Education in America."

43 Bailey et al., "A Blueprint for Back to School."

44 Bailey et al., "A Blueprint for Back to School," 11.

45 Bedrick and Ladner, "Let's Get Small: Microschools, Pandemic Pods, and the Future of Education in America."

46 Horn, "The Rapid Rise of Pandemic Pods," 3.

47 Welner, *Neovouchers*.

48 Molnar et al., *Virtual Schools in the U.S. 2021*.

49 Linda Darling-Hammond, *The Flat World and Education* (New York: Teachers College Press, 2010).

50 Bedrick and Ladner, "Let's Get Small: Microschools, Pandemic Pods, and the Future of Education in America," 8.

51 H. Potter, "Do Private School Vouchers Pose a Threat to Integration," The Century Foundation, March 21, 2017, retrieved December 15, 2021, from https://tcf.org/content/report/private-school-vouchers-pose-threat -integration/; William J. Mathis and Kevin G. Welner, *Do Choice Policies Segregate Schools?* (Boulder, CO: National Education Policy Center, March

2016), http://nepc.colorado.edu/files/publications/Mathis%20RBOPM-3 %20Choice%20Segregation.pdf.

52 See the Graduation Alliance/Engage New Mexico White paper at: https:// www.graduationalliance.com/wp-content/uploads/2020/06/NMPED-GA -White-Paper-June-2020.pdf.

53 New Mexico Public Education Department, "Press Release: Nearly 16,000 NM Students Got Free Academic Coaching Last Year," July 2, 2021, retrieved September 27, 2021, from https://webnew.ped.state.nm.us/news -releases/.

54 See the Graduation Alliance/Engage New Mexico White paper at https://www.graduationalliance.com/wp-content/uploads/2020/06 /NMPED-GA-White-Paper-June-2020.pdf See also A.I. Guzman, "You've Reached 17,494 Students Please Leave a Message," *Searchlight New Mexico,* August 18, 2021, retrieved September 27, 2021, from https://searchlightnm.org/utah-company-paid-millions-to-contact-nm -students/.

55 Guzman, "You've Reached 17,494 Students Please Leave a Message."

56 Horn, "The Rapid Rise of Pandemic Pods," 3; Bedrick and Ladner, "Let's Get Small: Microschools, Pandemic Pods, and the Future of Education in America," 11.

57 Carnoy, "School Vouchers Are Not a Proven Strategy for Improving Student Achievement"; Welner, *Neovouchers.*

58 Stanley Aronowitz, *Against Schooling: For an Education That Matters* (Boulder: Paradigm, 2008); Giroux, *Theory and Resistance in Education*; Freire, *Pedagogy of the Oppressed.*

59 Spring, *The Economization of Education.*

60 Means, *Learning to Save the Future.*

61 Sadowski, "When Data is Capital," 1–12.

62 Williamson and Piattoeva, "Objectivity as Standardization in Data-scientific Education Policy, Technology, and Governance," 64–76.

63 Despite disregarding student subjectivity and the social context, educational technology companies frequently misrepresent their products as "personalized" by virtue of being "adaptive." See the discussion of this with regard to Chan Zuckerberg's Summit Learning in Saltman, *The Swindle of Innovative Educational Finance.* See also Heather Roberts-Mahoney, Alexander Means, and Mark Garrison, "Netflixing

Human Capital Development: Personalized Learning Technology in the Corporatization of K–12 Education," *Journal of Education Policy* 31, no. 4 (2016): 1–16.

64 To see a number of examples of the convergence of educational technology with social emotional learning programs, see the website of the New Schools Venture Fund: www.newschools.org.

65 Saltman, *The Swindle of Innovative Educational Finance*; Boninger et al., "Personalized Learning and the Digital Privatization of Curriculum and Teaching"; Sadowski, "When Data is Capital."

66 David Berliner, "Kids Missing School Don't Worry," Dianeravitch.net May 28, 2020, retrieved September 27, 2021, from https://dianeravitch.net /2020/05/28/david-berliner-kids-missing-school-dont-worry/; Kevin G. Welner, David R. Garcia, and Lorrie Shepard, "NEPC Research Panel: Are Students 'Behind' as a Result of School Closures and Reliance on Remote Education?," September 25, 2020, retrieved September 20, 2021, from https://nepc.colorado.edu/publication/fyi-video-garcia-shepard.

67 Williamson et al., "Covid-19 Controversies and Critical Research in Digital Education," 124.

68 Gramsci, *Selections from the Prison Notebooks*, 3–23.

69 The dialogic versus monologic nature of education and culture is explained by a number of thinkers, including Paulo Friere, John Dewey, Stuart Hall, Jurgen Habermas, Lev Vygotsky, Mikhail Baktin, and Henry Giroux.

70 Kenneth J. Saltman and Alexander Means, "From Data-Driven to Democracy-Driven Educational Leadership," in *The Wiley International Handbook of Educational Leadership,* ed. Duncan Waite and Ira Bogotch (New York: Wiley Blackwell, 2017); Henry A. Giroux, *America's Education Deficit and the War on Youth: Reform Beyond Electoral Politics* (New York: Monthly Review Press, 2013); John Dewey, *Democracy and Education* (New York: Macmillan, 1916); Noam Chomsky, *Chomsky on Democracy and Education* (New York: Routledge, 2003); Amy Gutmann, *Democratic Education* (Princeton: Princeton University Press, 1987); Michael Apple, *Official Knowledge: Democratic Education in a Conservative Age* (New York: Routledge, 2014); Joel Westheimer, *What Kind of Citizen? Educating Our Children for the Common Good* (New York: Teachers College Press, 2015).

71 A sample includes Dewey, *Democracy and Education*; Henry Giroux, *On Critical Pedagogy* (New York: Bloomsbury, 2011); Gloria Ladson-Billings, *Culturally Relevant Pedagogy* (New York: Teachers College Press, 2021); Westheimer, *What Kind of Citizen?*

72 Dewey, *Democracy and Education*; Chomsky, *Chomsky on Democracy and Education*; Gutmann, *Democratic Education*; Aronowitz, *Against Schooling*; Giroux, *On Critical Pedagogy*; Ladson-Billings, *Culturally Relevant Pedagogy*; Westheimer, *What Kind of Citizen?*

73 Giroux, *On Critical Pedagogy*; Ladson-Billings, *Culturally Relevant Pedagogy*.

Chapter 4

1 Valerie Strauss, "Privatization of Public Education, Gaining Ground Report Says," *Washington Post*, April 18, 2022, retrieved November 30, 2022, from https://www.washingtonpost.com/education/2022/04/18/privatization-of-public-education-gaining-ground/.

2 Couldry and Mejias, *The Costs of Connection*.

3 Saltman, *The Failure of Corporate School Reform*.

4 Andre M. Perry, "How Charter Schools Are Prolonging Segregation," Brookings Institution, December 11, 2017, retrieved December 18, 2022, from https://www.brookings.edu/blog/the-avenue/2017/12/11/how-charter-schools-are-prolonging-segregation/; Adam Kho and Andrew McEachin, "A Descriptive Analysis of Cream Skimming and Pushout in Choice Versus Traditional School," *Education Finance and Policy* 17, no. 1 (2022): 160–87; Daniel J. Losen, Michael A. Keith II, Cheri L. Hodson, and Tia E. Martinez, "Charter Schools, Civil Rights and School Discipline," The Civil Rights Project, March 15, 2016, retrieved December 18, 2022, from https://www.civilrightsproject.ucla.edu/resources/projects/center-for-civil-rights-remedies/school-to-prison-folder/federal-reports/charter-schools-civil-rights-and-school-discipline-a-comprehensive-review/losen-et-al-charter-school-discipline-review-2016.pdf.

5 'Charter Schools in Perspective' Spencer Foundation and Public Agenda available at http://www.in-perspective.org/pages/teachers-and-teaching-at-charter-schools.

6 Saltman, *The Swindle of Innovative Educational Finance.*

7 Bruce Baker, "We Bought It Twice But We No Longer Own It: The Bad Public Policy behind Charter Real Estate Deals," School Finance 101, July 21, 2015, blog available at https://schoolfinance101.wordpress.com/2015 /07/21/we-bought-it-twice-but-we-no-longer-own-it-is-co-location-the -better-option/.

8 Sally Ho, "Exclusive: Billionaires Fuel Charter School Movement," *AP*, July 16, 2018, retrieved June 23, 2022, from https://apnews.com/article/ melinda-gates-north-america-education-wa-state-wire-tx-state-wire-92d c914dd97c487a9b9aa4b006909a8c.

9 Pauline Lipman, *The New Political Economy of Urban Education* (New York: Routledge, 2011).

10 Megen Feren, "Remote Learning and School Reopenings: What Worked and What Didn't," *Center for American Progress*, July 6, 2021, https://www .americanprogress.org/issues/education-k-12/reports/2021/07/06/501221 /remote-learning-school-reopenings-worked-didnt/; Natasha Singer, "Learning Apps Have Boomed in the Pandemic. Now Here Comes the Real Test," *The New York Times*, March 17, 2021.

11 David Bank, "California Venture Fund Raises $25 Million for Charter Schools," *The Wall Street Journal*, April 10, 2002, B2.

12 James Flanigan, "Venture Capitalists Are Investing in Educational Reform," *The New York Times*, February 16, 2006, C6.

13 Jeff Archer, "Venture Fund Seeds School Innovations," *Education Week* 21, no. 32 (April 24, 2002): 2.

14 Archer, "Venture Fund Seeds School Innovations," 1.

15 Jamie Manolev, Anna Sullivan, and Roger Slee, "The Datafication of Discipline: Class Dojo, Surveillance and a Performative Classroom Culture," *Learning, Media and Technology* (December 14, 2018): 1–16.

16 Retrieved June 29, 2022, from https://ideas.classdojo.com/f/mindfulness -breathing/1.

17 Retrieved June 30, 2022, from https://www.centervention.com/social -emotional-learning-curriculum/.

18 Jean-Luc Nancy, "The Compearance: From the Existence of 'Communism' to the Community of 'Existence'," *Political Theory* 20, no. 3 (August 1992): 371–98; Nancy writes, "Anger is the political sentiment par excellence. It brings out the qualities of the inadmissible, the intolerable. It is a

refusal and a resistance that with one step goes beyond all that can be accomplished reasonably—in order to open possible paths for a new negotiation of the reasonable but also paths of an uncompromising vigilance" (371).

19 Devin Coldewey, "Amira Learning Raises $11 Million to Put It's AI-powered Literacy Tutor in Post-Covid Classrooms," *Techcrunch*, April 14, 2021, retrieved July 6, 2022, from https://techcrunch.com /2021/04/14/amira-learning-raises-11m-to-put-its-ai-powered-literacy -tutor-in-post-covid-classrooms/?guccounter=1&guce_referrer=aHR 0cHM6Ly93d3cuZ29vZ2xlLmNvbS8&guce_referrer_sig=AQAAABc FQK5JkLHzDw963vn9laU_wzOR02zpQ9yiikB4QK7RsHKkrG1YH8I on58R9OrD_P9gXqLAlTpcZg4iyikEeIwJ-pXOJeCqyEZpnBDRyMx -WyqlqoWCOE6kj1bNMyQrvteN6iuXWGjBekIj8rQ2FlEboYEUgG -UbzqInarAGgqj.

20 See for example, Judy Trotti, Randy Hendricks, and Christie Bledsoe, "Emergent Literacy Development and Computer-Assisted Instruction," *SRATE Journal* 26, no. 1 (Winter 2017): 30–9.

21 Rod Berger, "Amira Learning CEO Personalizes Artificial Intelligence for Literacy Gains," *Forbes*, December 16, 2021, retrieved July 6, 2022, from https://www.forbes.com/sites/rodberger/2021/12/16/amira -learning-ceo-personalizes-artificial-intelligence-for-literacy-gains/?sh =2a8d191d1481.

22 Lipman, *The New Political Economy of Urban Education*.

23 Saltman, *The Failure of Corporate School Reform*.

24 Kevin Bushweller, "How Personalized Learning Is Weathering Tough Times," *Education Week* 40, no. 12 (November 4, 2020): 22–3.

25 Means, *Learning to Save the Future*; Dyer-Witheford et al., *Inhuman Power: Artificial Intelligence and the Future of Capitalism*.

26 Heidi Stevens, "The Chicago Tribune," May 2, 2018, 1.

27 Chicago Board of Education website contains archived contracts with Leap Innovations and other contractors cpsboe.org.

28 Leapinnovations.org.

29 Leapinnovations.org.

30 Leapinnovations.org.

31 Shoshana Zuboff, *The Age of Surveillance Capitalism* (New York: PublicAffairs, 2019).

32 Michele Molnar, "8 'Red Flags' to Look for in Products," *Education Week*, October 19, 2016, V36i9, 29–30.

33 Leapinnovations.org.

34 Leapinnovations.org.

35 Leapinnovations.org.

36 Henry Giroux makes these points in a number of places. See, for example, *Border Crossings: Cultural Workers and the Politics of Education*, 2nd Edition.

Chapter 5

1 This quote is from Prachi Naik, "When Trauma-Informed Pedagogy Is Not Enough: The Need for Increased School-Based Mental Health Services in Public Schools," Harvardkennedyschoolreview.com XIX (2019): 66–69. The Adverse Childhood Experiences study narrative can be found for example as well in Tom Brunzell, Lea Waters, and Helen Stokes, "Teacher Perspectives When Learning Trauma-Informed Practice Pedagogies: Stories of Meaning Making at Work," *Frontiers in Education* 7, no. 852228 (June 2022): 1–10; Jessica D. Cless and Briana S. Nelson Goff, "Teaching Trauma: A Model for Introducing Traumatic Materials in the Classroom," *Advances in Social Work* 18 (2017); Hal A. Lawson, James C. Caringi, Ruth Gottfried, Brian E. Bride, and Stephen P. Hydon, "Educators' Secondary Traumatic Stress, Children's Trauma, and the Need for Trauma Literacy," *Harvard Educational Review* 89, no. 3 (Fall 2019): 421–48.

2 One of many pieces of scholarship that typifies the "toxic stress" narrative is Jennifer Bashant, *Building a Trauma-Informed, Compassionate Classroom: Strategies and Activities to Reduce Challenging Behavior, Improve Learning Outcomes, and Increase Student Engagement* (Eau Claire: PESI, 2020). See in particular "Chapter 2: Withstanding the Elements During a Storm" part one, "Wired for Fear."

3 Bashant provides this list of app companies.

4 Naik, "When Trauma-Informed Pedagogy Is Not Enough: The Need for Increased School-Based Mental Health Services in Public Schools," 66–69.

5 Tom Brunzell, Lea Waters, and Helen Stokes, "Teacher Perspectives When Learning Trauma-Informed Practice Pedagogies: Stories of Meaning Making at Work," *Frontiers in Education* 7, no. 852228 (June 2022): 1–10.

6 Bashant, *Building a Trauma-Informed, Compassionate Classroom: Strategies and Activities to Reduce Challenging Behavior, Improve Learning Outcomes, and Increase Student Engagement*, 5.

7 Bashant, *Building a Trauma-Informed, Compassionate Classroom: Strategies and Activities to Reduce Challenging Behavior, Improve Learning Outcomes, and Increase Student Engagement*, 21.

8 See the important research of Teresa L. Sullivan, *The Educationalization of Student Emotional and Behaviroral Health* (New York: Palgrave Macmillan, 2018).

9 Bashant, *Building a Trauma-Informed, Compassionate Classroom: Strategies and Activities to Reduce Challenging Behavior, Improve Learning Outcomes, and Increase Student Engagement*, 95.

10 See for example, Barbara Ehrenreich, *Bright-Sided* (New York: Metropolitan Books, 2009) and Edgar Cabanas and Eva Illouz, *Manufacturing Happy Citizens: How the Science and Industry of Happiness Control Our Lives* (Medford, MA: Polity, 2019).

11 The "hidden curriculum" refers to the implicit lessons taught in schools that promote social relations and frameworks of meaning in the service of hegemonic power including the organization and production of knowledge and space in ways that naturalize and universalize the particular values of the ruling class. A partial list of theorists who have contributed to the concept include Michael Young, Basil Bernstein, Paul Willis, Bowles, and Gintis, *Schooling in Capitalist America*; Bourdieu and Passeron, *Social and Cultural Reproduction in Education*; Althusser, "Ideology and Ideological State Apparatuses: Notes Toward an Investigation"; Apple, *Ideology and Curriculum*; and Giroux, *Theory and Resistance in Education*.

12 Sadowski, "When Data Is Capital."

13 Will Self, "A Posthumous Shock: How Everything Became Trauma," *Harper's*, December, 2021, retrieved September 27, 2022, from https://harpers.org/archive/2021/12/a-posthumous-shock-trauma-studies-modernity-how-everything-became-trauma/.

14 Self explains the "ubiquity of traumatogenic technologies in our societies: those of specularity and acceleration, which render us simultaneously unreflective and frenetic." Such a conception of contemporary trauma leaves little room for the capacity for ideological analysis of trauma forestalling the possibilities of reconceptualizing experience by shifting frameworks of interpretation. As I discuss herein the possibility of critical engagement with traumatic experience demands a recognition of the pedagogical formation of subjectivity and the possibility of critical engagement to transform consciousness.

15 See Gail Bederman, *Manliness and Civilization* (Chicago: University of Chicago Press, 1995), for an excellent history and analysis of the gendered and racialized discourses of recapitulation theory and youth development. Nancy Lesko, *Act Your Age* (New York: Routledge, 2001) provides an excellent situating of this history in the development of adolescence and middle-level education in the field of education. Enora Brown and I discuss this as well in Enora Brown and Kenneth J. Saltman, eds., *The Critical Middle School Reader* (New York: Routledge, 2005).

16 DemocracyNow!, "Dr. Gabor Mate on 'The Myth of Normal' Healing in a Toxic Culture and How Capitalism Fuels Addiction," November 24, 2022 available at https://www.democracynow.org/2022/11/24/dr_gabor _mate_on_the_myth.

17 DemocracyNow!, "Dr. Gabor Mate."

18 Post-structural conceptions of selfhood are informed by the linguistic turn in cultural theory and de Sausaure's insights about the workings of language as a system of difference and the gap between signifiers and signified. Theories that further developed this include Lacanian psychoanalysis, Derridean deconstruction, and Foucault's discursive conception of self-formation; Stuart Hall's representational theory of culture brings these together. Work by Hall as well as by Ernesto Laclau and Chantal Mouffe, among others, bring together a post-structural conception of self with a post-structural conception of politics and culture stitching together theories of hegemonic change inspired by Gramsci. Henry Giroux has been the most significant and prolific educational theorist to develop the educative dimensions of politics and culture appropriating from the post-structural tradition.

10 See Erich Fromm, *Escape from Freedom* (1941; New York: Holt, 1994), and Paulo Freire's use of Fromm's psychology in *Pedagogy of the Oppressed.*

Chapter 6

1 This list of democratic characteristics, for example, is measured by the Democracy Index published by the Economist Intelligence Unit.

2 Democracy Index, Economist Intelligence Unit.

3 Sheldon Wolin, *Democracy, Incorporated* (Princeton: Princeton University Press, 2008); Henry A. Giroux, *Insurrections: Education in an Age of Counter Revolutionary Politics* (New York: Bloomsbury, 2023).

4 Hannah Natanson, Clara Ence Morse, and Anu Narayanswami, "An Explosion of Culture War Laws Is Changing Schools. Here's How," *The Washington Post*, October 18, 2022, https://www.washingtonpost.com/education/2022/10/18/education-laws-culture-war/.

5 Natanson, Morse, and Narayanswami, "An Explosion of Culture War Laws Is Changing Schools. Here's How."

6 I discuss at length the educational preconditions for contemporary conspiracy theory in Saltman, *The Alienation of Fact.*

7 Aronowitz, *Against Schooling.*

8 Bowles and Gintis, *Schooling in Capitalist America.*

9 Robin DiAngelo is the exemplar here. A diversity training Linkedin Learning Class, "Confronting Racism with Robin DiAngelo," at Coca-Cola included her claim, "To be less white is to: be less oppressive, less arrogant, less certain, less defensive, less ignorant, more humble." DiAngelo asked viewers to "break with white solidarity." Poppy Noor, "So Your Company Uses Diversity Training. Does It Even Work?" *The Guardian*, March 10, 2021, retrieved December 19, 2022, from https://www.theguardian.com/world/2021/mar/10/workplace-diversity-training-does-it-work-racial-justice.
The point not to be missed is that DiAngelo has made an industry of conflating whiteness as an identity position with white supremacy as an ideology, thereby undermining the articulation of white identity through anti-racist ideals and solidarity with other emancipatory struggles. Instead,

she articulates white identity as a position of guilt and shame. This both essentializes racial identity and fuels white supremacist defensiveness and pride in white identity as innocent, pure, and victimized. The Coca-Cola training and denunciation of this form of anti-racism was pounced upon by right-wing media as evidence that anti-racism itself is really a form of anti-white racism rather than recognizing that anti-racism is crucial for societies committed to democratic values and requires multiracial solidarity. As Keeanga Yamahta-Taylor, *From #Blacklives Matter to Black Liberation* (Chicago: Haymarket, 2016), 215 put it, "solidarity is standing in unity with people even when you have not personally experienced their particular oppression." See Henry A. Giroux, *Channel Surfing: Race Talk and the Destruction of Today's Youth* (New York: Palgrave Macmillan, 1997), for an important discussion of the pitfalls of racial essentialism and the need for pedagogies of anti-racist whiteness.

References

Althusser, Louis, "Ideology and Ideological State Apparatuses: Notes Toward an Investigation." In *Lenin and Philosophy and Other Essays*, 85–126. New York: Monthly Review Press, 2001.

"American Academy of Pediatrics Website healthychildren.org 'Where We Stand: Screen Time.'" Retrieved December 14, 2021, from https://www.healthychildren.org/English/family-life/Media/Pages/Where-We-Stand-TV-Viewing-Time.aspx?_gl=1*152d12x*_ga*ODU0NzUxMDA0LjE2Mzk1MDE3MjI.*_ga_FD9D3XZVQQ*MTYzOTUwMTcyMS4xLjEuMTYzOTUwMTk1My4w&_ga=2.131480847.1074417706.1639501722-854751004.1639501722.

Anyon, Jean, *Radical Possibilities*. New York: Routledge, 2005.

Apple, Michael, *Ideology and Curriculum*. New York: Routledge, 1977.

Apple, Michael, *Official Knowledge: Democratic Education in a Conservative Age*. New York: Routledge, 2014.

Archer, Jeff, "Venture Fund Seeds School Innovations." *Education Week* 21, no. 32 (2002): 1–8.

Aronowitz, Stanley, *Against Schooling: For an Education that Matters*. Boulder: Paradigm, 2008.

Bailey, J.P., F.M. Hess, C. Cerf, C. Conaway, S. El-Mekki, D. Erquiaga, K. Henderson, D. Klussmann, W. Lewis, P. Lockett, C. McQueen, K. Rausch, N. Rees, G. Robinson, A. Rotherham, I. Rowe, I. Scott, H. Skandera, D. Steiner, J. Weiss, and J.J. White, "A Blueprint for Back to School." American Enterprise Institute. May 4, 2020. Retrieved September 27, 2021, from https://www.aei.org/research-products/report/a-blueprint-for-back-to-school/.

Baker, Bruce, "We Bought It Twice But We No Longer Own It: The Bad Public Policy Behind Charter Real Estate Deals' School Finance 101." July 21, 2015 blog. Retrieved from https://schoolfinance101.wordpress.com/2015/07/21/we-bought-it-twice-but-we-no-longer-own-it-is-co-location-the-better-option/.

Bank, David, "California Venture Fund Raises $25 Million for Charter Schools." *The Wall Street Journal*, April 10, 2002.

Bashant, Jennifer, *Building a Trauma-Informed, Compassionate Classroom: Strategies and Activities to Reduce Challenging Behavior, Improve Learning Outcomes, and Increase Student Engagement*. Eau Claire: PESI, 2020.

Bauman, Zygmunt, *In Search of Politics*. Stanford: Stanford University Press, 1999.

Beck, Ulrich, *Risk Society: Towards a New Modernity*. Thousand Oaks: Sage, 1992.

Becker, Gary, *Human Capital*. Chicago: University of Chicago Press, 1964.

Bederman, Gail, *Manliness and Civilization*. Chicago: University of Chicago Press, 1995.

Bedrick, J., and M. Ladner, "Let's Get Small: Microschools, Pandemic Pods, and the Future of Education in America." The Heritage Foundation Center for Education Policy No. 3540, October 6, 2020. Retrieved September 27, 2021, from https://www.heritage.org/education/report/lets-get-small -microschools-pandemic-pods-and-the-future-education-america.

Berger, Rod, "Amira Learning CEO Personalizes Artificial Intelligence for Literacy Gains." *Forbes*, December 16, 2021. Retrieved July 6, 2022, from https://www.forbes.com/sites/rodberger/2021/12/16/amira-learning-ceo -personalizes-artificial-intelligence-for-literacy-gains/?sh=2a8d191d1481.

Berliner, David, "Kids Missing School Don't Worry." Dianeravitch.net. May 28, 2020. Retrieved September 27, 2021, from https://dianeravitch.net /2020/05/28/david-berliner-kids-missing-school-dont-worry/.

Boninger, Faith, Alex Molnar, and C. Saldana, "Personalized Learning and the Digital Privatization of Curriculum and Teaching." *National Education Policy Center*, April 2019. Retrieved February 3, 2020, from http://nepc .colorado.edu/publication/personalized-learning.

Bourdieu, Pierre, and Jean Passeron, *Social and Cultural Reproduction in Education*. Thousand Oaks: Sage, 1992.

Bowles, Samuel, and Herbert Gintis, *Schooling in Capitalist America*. 1976; Chicago: Haymarket, 2011.

Bracey, Gerald, "Knowledge Universe and Virtual Schools: Educational Breakthrough or Digital Raid on the Public Treasury?" Education Policy Studies Laboratory, 2004. https://nepc.colorado.edu/publication/ knowledge-universe-and-virtual-schools-educational-breakthrough-or -digital-raid-public-t.

Brown, Enora, and Kenneth J. Saltman (eds.), *The Critical Middle School Reader*. New York: Routledge, 2005.

Brunzell, Tom, Lea Waters, and Helen Stokes, "Teacher Perspectives When Learning Trauma-Informed Practice Pedagogies. Stories of Meaning Making at Work." *Frontiers in Education* 7, no. 852228 (June 2022): 1–10.

Bushweller, Kevin, "How Personalized Learning is Weathering Tough Times." *Education Week* 40, no. 12 (November 4, 2020): 22–23.

Butrymowicz, S., "Education Companies See an 'Upside to the Pandemic' for Business." *Hechinger Report*, June 18, 2020.

Cabanas, Edgar, and Eva Illouz, *Manufacturing Happy Citizens: How the Science and Industry of Happiness Control Our Lives*. Medford: Polity, 2019.

Capitalism Hits the Fan (2008) film Dir. Media Education Foundation.

Carnoy, Martin, "School Vouchers are not a Proven Strategy for Improving Student Achievement." *Economic Policy Institute*, February 28, 2017. Retrieved from http://www.epi.org/publication/school-vouchers-are-not-a-proven-strategy-for-improving-student-achievement/.

Catalano, Frank, "Pandemic Spurs Changes in the Edtech Schools Use, from the Classroom to the Admin Office." *EdSurge*, January 26, 2021. Retrieved December 13, 2021, from https://www.edsurge.com/news/2021-01-26-pandemic-spurs-changes-in-the-edtech-schools-use-from-the-classroom-to-the-admin-office.

Chandler, David, and Julian Reid, *The Neoliberal Subject: Resilience, Adaptation, and Vulnerability*. New York: Rowman & Littlefield, 2016.

Charpignon, Marie-Laure, Johnattan Ontiveros, Saahil Sundaresan, et al. "Evaluation of Suicides Among US Adolescents During the Covid-19 Pandemic." *JAMA Network* 176, no. 7 (2022): 724–726.

"Charter Schools in Perspective." Spencer Foundation and Public Agenda. Retrieved from http://www.in-perspective.org/pages/teachers-and-teaching-at-charter-schools.

Chomsky, Noam, *Chomsky on Democracy and Education*. New York: Routledge, 2003.

Cless, Jessica D., and Briana S. Nelson Goff, "Teaching Trauma: A Model for Introducing Traumatic Materials in the Classroom." *Advances in Social Work* 18, no. 1 (2017): 25–38.

Coldewey, Devin, "Amira Learning Raises $11 Million to Put It's AI-powered Literacy Tutor in Post-Covid Classrooms." *Techcrunch*, April 14, 2021. Retrieved July 6, 2022, from https://techcrunch.com/2021/04/14/amira-learning-raises-11m-to-put-its-ai-powered-literacy-tutor-in-post-covid-.

Couldry, Nick, and Ulises A. Mejias, *The Costs of Connection: How Data is Colonizing Human Life and Appropriating it for Capitalism*. Stanford: Stanford University Press, 2019.

Cramond, Bonnie, "Appendix: Choosing a Creativity Assessment That is Fit For Purpose." The Lego Foundation.

Darling-Hammond, Linda, *The Flat World and Education*. New York: Teachers College Press, 2010.

Democracy Index, Economist Intelligence Unit.

DemocracyNow!, "Dr. Gabor Mate on 'The Myth of Normal' Healing in a Toxic Culture and How Capitalism Fuels Addiction." November 24, 2022. Retrieved from https://www.democracynow.org/2022/11/24/dr_gabor _mate_on_the_myth.

Dewey, John, *Democracy and Education*. New York: Macmillan, 1916.

Duckworth, Angela, "TED Talk 'Grit: The Power of Passion and Perseverance'." May 9, 2013.

Dyer-Witheford, Nick, Atle Mikkola Kjosen, and James Steinhoff, *Inhuman Power: Artificial Intelligence and the Future of Capitalism* London: Pluto Press, 2019.

Education Week, "The Coronavirus Spring: The Historic Closing of U.S. Schools (A Timeline)." July 1, 2020. Retrieved December 14, 2021, from https://www.edweek.org/leadership/the-coronavirus-spring-the-historic -closing-of u s-schools-a-timeline/2020/07.

Ehrenreich, Barbara, *Bright-Sided*. New York: Metropolitan Books, 2009.

Evans, Brad, and Julian Reid. *Resilient Life: The Art of Living Dangerously*. Malden: Polity Press, 2014.

FEMA, "Crisis Response and Disaster Resilience 2030: Forging Strategic Response in an Age of Uncertainty." January, 2012.

Feren, Megen, "Remote Learning and School Reopenings: What Worked and What Didn't." *Center for American Progress*, July 6, 2021. Retrieved from https://www.americanprogress.org/issues/education-k-12/reports/2021/07 /06/501221/remote-learning-school-reopenings-worked-didnt/.

Flanigan, James, "Venture Capitalists are Investing in Educational Reform." *The New York Times*, February 16, 2006.

Fraser, Nancy, "From Discipline to Flexibilization: Rereading Foucault in the Shadow of Globalization." *Constellations* 10, no. 2 (2003): 160–171.

Fraser, Nancy, *Cannibal Capitalism*. New York: Verso, 2022.

Freire, Paulo, *Pedagogy of the Oppressed*. New York: Continuum, 1972.

Friedman, Milton, *Capitalism and Freedom*. Chicago: University of Chicago Press, 1962.

Giroux, Henry A., *Theory and Resistance in Education*. Westport: Bergin & Garvey, 1983.

Giroux, Henry A., *Channel Surfing: Race Talk and the Destruction of Today's Youth*. New York: Palgrave Macmillan, 1997.

Giroux, Henry A., *The Mouse that Roared: Disney and the End of Innocence*. Lanham: Rowman & Littlefield, 1999.

Giroux, Henry A., *Stealing Innocence: Youth, Corporate Power, and the Politics of Culture*. New York: Palgrave Macmillan, 2000.

Giroux, Henry A., *Border Crossings, 2nd Edition*. New York: Routledge, 2005.

Giroux, Henry A., *America's Education Deficit and the War on Youth: Reform Beyond Electoral Politics*. New York: Monthly Review Press, 2013.

Giroux, Henry A., *On Critical Pedagogy, 2nd Edition*. New York: Bloomsbury, 2020.

Giroux, Henry A., *Insurrections: Education in an Age of Counter Revolutionary Politics*. New York: Bloomsbury, 2023.

Goodman, Robin Truth, and Kenneth J. Saltman, *Strange Love: Or How We Learn to Stop Worrying and Love the Market*. Lanham: Rowman & Littlefield, 2002.

Graduation Alliance/Engage New Mexico White Paper. Retrieved from https://www.graduationalliance.com/wp-content/uploads/2020/06/NMPED-GA-White-Paper-June-2020.pdf.

Gramsci, Antonio, *Selections from the Prison Notebooks* (ed. Quinton Hoare). New York: International Publishers, 1971.

Gutmann, Amy, *Democratic Education*. Princeton: Princeton University Press, 1987.

Guzman, A.I., "You've Reached 17,494 Students Please Leave a Message." *Searchlight New Mexico*, August 18, 2021. Retrieved September 27, 2021, from https://searchlightnm.org/utah-company-paid-millions-to-contact-nm-students/.

Harvey, David, *A Brief History of Neoliberalism*. Oxford: Oxford University Press, 2007.

Ho, Sally, "Exclusive: Billionaires Fuel Charter School Movement." *AP*, July 16, 2018. Retrieved June 23, 2022, from https://apnews.com/article/melinda-gates-north-america-education-wa-state-wire-tx-state-wire-92dc914dd97c487a9b9aa4b006909a8c.

Horn, M.B., "The Rapid Rise of Pandemic Pods." *Education Next* 21, no. 1 (2021): 3. Retrieved September 27, 2021, from https://www.educationnext .org/rapid-rise-pandemic-pods-will-parent-response-covid-19-lead-to -lasting-changes/

Hursh, David, *High Stakes Testing and the Decline of Teaching and Learning.* Lanham: Rowman & Littlefield, 2008.

Hursh, David, *The End of Public Schools: The Corporate Reform Agenda to Privatize Education.* New York: Routledge, 2015.

Hursh, David, Jeanette Deutermann, Lisa Rudley, Zhe Chen, and Sarah McGinnis, *Opting Out: The Story of the Parents' Grassroot Movement to Achieve Whole Child Public Schools.* Gorham: Meyers Educational Press, 2020.

Intergovernmental Panel on Climate Change (IPCC), "2021: Summary for Policymakers." In *Climate Change 2021: The Physical Science Basis. Contribution of Working Group I to the Sixth Assessment Report of the Intergovernmental Panel on Climate Change*, eds. V. Masson-Delmotte, P. Zhai, A. Pirani, S.L. Connors, C. Péan, S. Berger, N. Caud, Y. Chen, L. Goldfarb, M.I. Gomis, M. Huang, K. Leitzell, E. Lonnoy, J.B.R. Matthews, T.K. Maycock, T. Waterfield, O. Yelekçi, R. Yu, and B. Zhou. Cambridge: Cambridge University Press. In Press.

Klein, Naomi, *The Shock Doctrine.* New York: Metropolitan Books, 2007.

Klein, Naomi, *The Battle for Paradise.* Chicago: Haymarket Books, 2018.

Kho, Adam, and Andrew McEachin, "A Descriptive Analysis of Cream Skimming and Pushout in Choice Versus Traditional School." *Education Finance and Policy* 17, no. 1 (2022): 160–187.

Kovacs, Philip (ed.), *The Gates Foundation and the Future of U.S. Public Schools.* New York: Routledge, 2011.

Kwek, Glenda, "Brains and Bracelets: Gates Funds Wrist Sensors for Students." *The Sydney Morning Herald*, June 14, 2012.

Ladson-Billings, Gloria, *Culturally Relevant Pedagogy.* New York: Teachers College Press, 2021.

Lawson, Hal A., James C. Caringi, Ruth Gottfried, Brian E. Bride, and Stephen P. Hydon, "Educators' Secondary Traumatic Stress, Children's Trauma, and the Need for Trauma Literacy." *Harvard Educational Review* 89, no. 3 (Fall 2019): 421–48.

The Lego Foundation, "'Assessing Creativity: A Palette of Possibilities'; The Pedagogy of Play Research Team, 'Playful Participatory Research: An Emerging Methodology for Developing a Pedagogy of Play' A Project Zero

Working Paper [Project Zero at Harvard Graduate School of Education/ International School at Billund Funded by Lego Foundation], July 2016

The Lego Foundation, "What We Mean by: Creativity" ['leaflet'].

The Lego Foundation, "Creating Systems: How Can Education Systems Reform to Enhance Learners' Creativity?" Creativity Matters No. 2.

Lesko, Nancy, *Act Your Age*. New York: Routledge, 2001.

Li, David K., "Youth Suicide Attempts Soared During Pandemic, CDC Report Says." *NBC News*, June 11, 2021.

Life and Debt (2001) dir. Stephanie Black.

Lipman, Pauline, *The New Political Economy of Urban Education*. New York: Routledge, 2011.

Locke, John, *An Essay Concerning Human Understanding*. 1690; Oxford: Oxford University Press, 1798.

Losen, Daniel J., Michael A. Keith II, Cheri L. Hodson, and Tia E. Martinez, "Charter Schools, Civil Rights and School Discipline." The Civil Rights Project, March 15, 2016. Retrieved December 18, 2022, from https:// www.civilrightsproject.ucla.edu/resources/projects/center-for-civil-rights -remedies/school-to-prison-folder/federal-reports/charter-schools-civil -rights-and-school-discipline-a-comprehensive-review/losen-et-al-charter -school-discipline-review-2016.pdf.

Macedo, Donaldo, *Literacies of Power*. New York: Westview, 2006.

Mandell, Ben, Daniel Wilson, Jen Ryan, Katie Ertel, Mara Drechevsky, and Megina Baker, "Towards a Pedagogy of Play: A Project Zero Working Paper." July 2016.

Manolev, Jamie, Anna Sullivan, and Roger Slee, "The Datafication of Discipline: Class Dojo, Surveillance and a Performative Classroom Culture." *Learning, Media and Technology* 44 (December 14, 2018): 1–16.

Mathis, William J., and Kevin G. Welner, *Do Choice Policies Segregate Schools?* Boulder: National Education Policy Center, March 2016. http:// nepc.colorado.edu/files/publications/Mathis%20RBOPM-3%20Choice %20Segregation.pdf.

McDowell, Alysson, "Wrench in the Gears (blog)." https://wrenchinthegears .com.

Mcelrath, K., "Nearly 93% of Households with School-Age Children Report Some Form of Distance Learning During Covid-19." August 20, 2020. Retrieved December 14, 2021, from https://www.census.gov/library/stories /2020/08/schooling-during-the-covid-19-pandemic.html.

McRobbie, Angela, "Top Girls?" *Cultural Studies* 21, no. 4–5 (2007): 718–737.

Means, Alexander J., *Schooling in the Age of Austerity*. New York: Palgrave Macmillan, 2013.

Means, Alexander J., *Learning to Save the Future*. New York: Routledge, 2018.

Mirowski, P., *Never Let a Serious Crisis Go to Waste*. New York: Verso, 2014.

Molnar, A., G. Miron, M.K. Barbour, L. Huerta, S.R. Shafer, J.K. Rice, A. Glover, N. Browning, S. Hagle, and F. Boninger, *Virtual Schools in the U.S. 2021*. Boulder: National Education Policy Center, 2021. Retrieved September 29, 2021, from http://nepc.colorado.edu/publication/virtual-schools-annual-2021.

Molnar, Michele, "8 'Red Flags' to Look for in Products." *Education Week*, October 19, 2016, V36i9, 29–30.

Monarrez, Tomas, Brian Kisida, and Matthew M. Chingos, "The Effect of Charter Schools on School Segregation." *EdWorkingPaper*: 20–308, 2020. Retrieved December 11, 2022, from Annenberg Institute at Brown University: https://doi.org/10.26300/1z61-br35.

Mouffe, Chantal, *For a Left Populism*. New York: Verso, 2019.

Mouffe, Chantal, *Towards a Green Democratic Revolution: Left Populism and the Power of Affects*. New York: Verso, 2022.

Naik, Prachi, "When Trauma-Informed Pedagogy Is Not Enough: The Need for Increased School-Based Mental Health Services in Public Schools." *Kennedy School Review* XIX (2019): 66–69. Harvardkennedyschoolreview.com.

Nancy, Jean-Luc, "The Compearance: From the Existence of 'Communism' to the Community of 'Existence.'" *Political Theory* 20 no. 3 (August 1992): 371–398.

Natanson, Hannah, Clara Ence Morse, Anu Narayanswami, and Christina Brause, "An Explosion of Culture War Laws is Changing Schools. Here's How." *The Washington Post*, October 18, 2022. https://www.washingtonpost.com/education/2022/10/18/education-laws-culture-war/.

Natasha Singer, "Learning Apps Have Boomed in the Pandemic. Now Here Comes the Real Test." *The New York Times*, March 17, 2021.

The National Security Strategy of the United States of America. (September 2002). Retrieved September 27, 2021, from https://georgewbush-whitehouse.archives.gov/nsc/nss/2002/.

New Mexico Public Education Department, "Press Release: Nearly 16,000 NM Students Got Free Academic Coaching Last Year." July 2, 2021. Retrieved September 27, 2021, from https://webnew.ped.state.nm.us/news-releases/.

Noor, Poppy, "So Your Company Uses Diversity Training. Does it Even Work?" *The Guardian*, March 10, 2021. Retrieved December 19, 2022, from https://www.theguardian.com/world/2021/mar/10/workplace -diversity-training-does-it-work-racial-justice.

OECD, "Skills for Social Progress." March 10, 2015. https://doi.org/10.1787 /23078731.

OECD, "Social and Emotional Skills: Well-Being, Connectedness, and Success." World Economic Forum. "Schools of the Future: Defining New Models of Education for the Fourth Industrial Revolution." January 2020, 1–33. www.weforum.org.

Parker, Rachel, and Bo Stjerne Thomsen, "Executive Summary: Learning Through Play at School." *White Paper Lego Foundation*, March 2019.

Pedroni, Thomas C., "Through Jean Anyon's 'Screen Door': The Differentially Racialized Incursion of the Neoliberal State in Milwaukee and Detroit Schools." *Teachers College Record* 123, no. 14 (2021): 115–128.

Perelman, Michael, *The Invention of Capitalism*. Durham: Duke University Press, 2000.

Perry, Andre M., "How Charter Schools Are Prolonging Segregation." *Brookings Institution*, December 11, 2017. Retrieved December 18, 2022, from https://www.brookings.edu/blog/the-avenue/2017/12/11/how -charter-schools-are-prolonging-segregation/.

Potter, H., "Do Private School Vouchers Pose a Threat to Integration." *The Century Foundation*, March 21, 2017. Retrieved December 15, 2021, from https://tcf.org/content/report/private-school-vouchers-pose-threat -integration/.

Robbins, Christopher, *Expelling Hope: The Assault on Youth and the Militarization of Schooling*. Albany: SUNY Press, 2009.

Roberts-Mahoney, Heather, Alexander Means, and Mark Garrison, "Netflixing Human Capital Development: Personalized Learning Technology in the Corporatization of K–12 Education." *Journal of Education Policy* 31, no. 4 (2016): 1–16.

Robinson, William I., *Into the Tempest*. Chicago: Haymarket, 2019.

Robinson, William I., *The Global Police State*. London: Pluto Press, 2020.

Rousseau, Jean Jacques, *Emile, or on Education*. 1763; New York: Basic Books, 1979.

Sadowski, Jathan, "When Data Is Capital: Datafication, Accumulation, and Extraction." *Big Data and Society* 6 (January–June 2019): 1–12.

Saltman, Kenneth J., *Collateral Damage: Corporatizing Schools—A Threat to Democracy*. Lanham: Rowman & Littlefield, 2000.

Saltman, Kenneth J., *The Edison Schools*. New York: Routledge, 2005.

Saltman, Kenneth J., *Capitalizing on Disaster: Taking and Breaking Public Schools*. New York: Routledge, 2007a.

Saltman, Kenneth J., *Schooling in Disaster Capitalism*. New York: Routledge, 2007b.

Saltman, Kenneth J., *The Gift of Education: Public Education and Venture Philanthropy*. New York: Palgrave, 2010.

Saltman, Kenneth J., and David Gabbard (eds.), *Education as Enforcement: The Militarization and Corporatization of Schools*, Second Edition. 2002; New York: Routledge, 2010.

Saltman, Kenneth J., *The Failure of Corporate School Reform*. New York: Routledge, 2012.

Saltman, Kenneth J., "The Austerity School: Grit, Character, and the Privatization of Education." *Symploke* 22 no. 1–2 (2014): 41–57.

Saltman, Kenneth J., "Corporate Schooling Meets Corporate Media: Standards, Testing, and Technophilia." *Review of Education Pedagogy Cultural Studies* 38, no. 2 (2016a): 105–23.

Saltman, Kenneth J., *Scripted Bodies: Corporate Power, Smart Technologies, and the Undoing of Public Education*. New York: Routledge, 2016b.

Saltman, Kenneth J., and Alexander Means, "From Data-Driven to Democracy-Driven Educational Leadership." In *The Wiley International Handbook of Educational Leadership*, eds. Duncan Waite, and Ira Bogotch, 125–37. New York: Wiley Blackwell, 2017.

Saltman, Kenneth J., *The Politics of Education: A Critical Introduction Second Edition*. New York: Routledge, 2018a.

Saltman, Kenneth J., *The Swindle of Innovative Educational Finance*. Minneapolis: University of Minnesota Press, 2018b.

Saltman, Kenneth J., *The Alienation of Fact: AI, Digital Educational Privatization and the False Promise of Bodies and Numbers*. Cambridge: MIT Press, 2022.

Self, Will, "A Posthumous Shock: How Everything Became Trauma." *Harper's*, December 2021.

Slater, Graham B., "The Precarious Subject of Neoliberal Education: Resilient Life in the Catastrophic Conjuncture." In *Handbook of Critical Approaches to Politics and Policy of Education*, eds. Kenneth J. Saltman, and Nicole Nguyen, 151–60. New York: Routledge, 2022.

Sociology is a Martial Art (2001) dir. Pierre Carles.

Spring, Joel, *The Economization of Education: Human Capital, Global Corporations, Skills-Based Schooling*. New York: Routledge, 2015.

Stevens, Heidi, "The Chicago Tribune." May 2, 2018, 1.

Strauss, Valerie, "Big Education Firms Spend Millions Lobbying for Pro-Testing Policies." *Washington Post*, March 30, 2015.

Strauss, Valerie, "Cuomo Questions Why School Buildings Still Exist—And Says New York Will Work With Bill Gates To 'Reimagine Education.'" *The Washington Post*, May 6, 2020.

Strauss, Valerie, "Privatization of Public Education, Gaining Ground Report Says." *The Washington Post*, April 18, 2022. Retrieved November 30, 2022, from https://www.washingtonpost.com/education/2022/04/18/privatization-of-public-education-gaining-ground/.

Sullivan, Teresa L., *The Educationalization of Student Emotional and Behavioral Health*. New York: Palgrave Macmillan, 2018.

Tierney, Kathleen, *The Social Roots of Risk: Producing Disasters, Promoting Resilience*. Stanford: Stanford University Press, 2014.

Tollefson, J., "Why Deforestation and Extinction Make Pandemics More Likely." *Nature*, August 7, 2020. Retrieved September 27, 2021, from https://www.nature.com/articles/d41586-020-02341-1.

Tough, Paul, *How Children Succeed: Grit, Curiosity, and the Hidden Power of Character*. New York: Houghton-Mifflin, 2012.

United States Department of Education Office of Civil Rights, "Education in a Pandemic: The Disparate Impact of Covid-19 on America's Students." Retrieved December 14, 2021, from https://www2.ed.gov/about/offices/list/ocr/docs/20210608-impacts-of-covid19.pdf.

Welner, Kevin, *Neovouchers: The Emergence of Tuition Tax Credits for Private Schooling*. Lanham: Rowman & Littlefield, 2008.

Welner, Kevin G., David R. Garcia, and Lorrie Shepard, "NEPC Research Panel: Are Students 'Behind' as a Result of School Closures and Reliance on Remote Education?" September 25, 2020. Retrieved September 20, 2021, from https://nepc.colorado.edu/publication/fyi-video-garcia-shepard.

Westheimer, Joel, *What Kind of Citizen? Educating Our Children for the Common Good*. New York: Teachers College Press, 2015.

Williamson, Ben, *Big Data in Education*. Thousand Oaks: Sage, 2017.

Williamson, Ben, and Nelli Piattoeva, "Objectivity as Standardization in Data-Scientific Education Policy, Technology, and Governance." *Learning, Media and Technology* 44, no. 1 (2019): 64–76. DOI: 10.1080/17439884.2018.1556215.

Williamson, Ben, and Anna Hogan, "The Edtech Pandemic Shock." *Education International*, July 10, 2020. Retrieved December 15, 2021, from https://www.ei-ie.org/en/item/23423:the-edtech-pandemic-shock-by-ben-williamson-anna-hogan.

Williamson, Ben, R. Eynon, and J. Potter, "Pandemic Politics, Pedagogies and Practices: Digital Technologies and Distance Education During the Coronavirus Emergency." *Learning, Media and Technology* 45, no. 2 (2020): 107–114. https://doi.org/10.1080/17439884.2020.1761641.

Williamson, Ben, F. Macgilchrist, and J. Potter, "Covid-19 Controversies and Critical Research in Digital Education." *Learning, Media and Technology* 46, no. 2 (2021): 117–127. https://doi.org/10.1080/17439884.2021.1922437.

Wolff, Richard D., and Stephen A. Resnick, *Contending Economic Theories: Neoclassical, Keynesian, and Marxian*. Cambridge: MIT Press, 2015.

Wolin, Sheldon, *Democracy, Incorporated*. Princeton: Princeton University Press, 2008.

World Economic Forum, "Schools of the Future: Defining New Models of Education for the Fourth Industrial Revolution." January, 2020.

World Economic Forum, "The Global Risks Report 2021." 2021 Retrieved September 27, 2021, from http://www3.weforum.org/docs/WEF_The_Global_Risks_Report_2021.pdf.

Yamahta-Taylor, Keeanga, *From #Blacklives Matter to Black Liberation*. Chicago: Haymarket, 2016.

Zuboff, Shoshana, *The Age of Surveillance Capitalism*. New York: PublicAffairs, 2019.

Index